Angel Blessings

Ani

To my loving husband, Joe, and my two angels,
Haley and Tess

HELIOTROPIA

www.mascotbooks.com

From Stilettos to Wings

The author has tried to recreate events, locales, and conversations from her memories of them. In order to maintain anonymity, in some instances, she may have changed the names of individuals and places or identifying characteristics and details.

Photography by Lauren Reid
Cover Model — Haley Dumas
Angel Illustrations by Christina Rosenthal

For more information, please contact:
Mascot Books
620 Herndon Parkway, Suite 320
Herndon, VA 20170
info@mascotbooks.com

Library of Congress Control Number: 2017911374

CPSIA Code: PROPM1117A
ISBN-13: 978-1-68401-450-7

Printed in the United States

From Stilettos To Wings

ANI EUSTICE

Contents

Prologue

I was guided to write this book when I began working with the angelic realm and channeling a group of angels that refer to themselves as "The Great Eloheim Beings." I call them the "White Angels," as that is how I see them. I guess it is fair to say that they were my inspiration and my co-authors. This book is an account of my journey from living an ordinary life to one guided and directed by angels. The motivation behind this book was merely the desire to illustrate that even the most mundane life can be a miraculous one. I knew that one day I would have to share the messages and guidance of the White Angels with others, and this is my attempt to do so. Their wisdom and revelations are written in bold letters on these pages so that you can easily distinguish between my words and theirs. I do not edit their words in order to maintain the purity of their information. I often use the word "God" in this book to describe the Divine All; however, please feel free to substitute any word that resonates with you. It is my wish that you will be enlightened by the words of the White Angels and understand that we all have access to these Divine Eloheim Beings of Light.

Ani
June 4, 2017

Chapter 1

Angels

OLYEON

"I communicate to you in nature.
This is where you find your peace."

"Angels are divine beings created to help humankind
and the universe. Our primary responsibility is to
lead humankind to the light and assist with their
expansion."
—The White Angels

Angels are divine messengers of God. They are non-gender light beings too numerous to count, who vibrate to the frequency of unconditional love. Angels have been referenced in many diverse religious texts and have appeared throughout the centuries to saints and prophets of all religions. The Catholic priest and philosopher Saint Thomas Aquinas wrote, "Angels transcend every religion, every philosophy, every creed. In fact, angels have no religion as we know it..."

Angels are here to help heal, guide, and protect you. Believing and trusting in their existence is the first step in accessing their divine guidance. Though we cannot see them, they are nearby. The Angelic Realm coexists simultaneously with our world.

I like to use the analogy of a glass bottom boat. The Angelic Realm is the glass bottom boat, the angels are the people in the boat, and we are the fish in the water underneath. The angels are near us and yet we are separated. We cannot see them but they can see us.

Just as the fish might sense the movement of the boat and the vibration it makes upon the water, we too can sense if our angels are near. It is up to us to keep our vibrations high so that we can feel the angels around us. The only thing separating us is the rate at which we vibrate. Frequency of vibration is the glass in the boat separating us from the angels.

I began communicating with angels later in my life. Although they vibrate at higher frequencies, it has been my experience that each angel has a different energy. Some angels feel bold and powerful, while others feel soft and gentle. I have even worked with angels that are quite funny.

The first angel that came to me was my Guardian Angel Johannson. Johannson opened up an opportunity, and soon I was communing with angels on a regular basis. In addition to working with guardian angels, I began channeling the White Angels.

I believe each one of us has the ability to communicate directly with angels. It is a matter of raising our awareness and expanding our consciousness. It is important to release any old beliefs that we are not "worthy" enough or that only saints and prophets have exclusivity to the angelic realm. Communicating with angels requires faith and trust. Angels were created to assist humankind and guide us to fulfill our life purpose, so why wouldn't we have direct access to them?

The White Angels appear as magnificent beings of light. They refer to themselves as the "Great Eloheim Beings." They are a collective group with one voice. I call them the White Angels because that is how I see them—as beautiful light beings of white. They come in and out, like a cloud or mist of white, and I feel surrounded by their energy.

"We are a group of celestial beings helping you spread love and light to the world. We are eager for you to bring awareness to others of our existence and desire that you share our messages. Our primary responsibility is to lead humankind to the light and assist with the expansion this planet and humankind. We work through energy fields and vibrations, downloading thoughts and aha moments through synchronicities. It is important to keep your vibrations high so that we can be more accessible to you. We are ever-present and ever-near."

— The White Angels

Unlike my communication with guardian angels, the White Angels' message is not specific to one individual, but is intended to be shared with the collective.

> "Our communication is direct and precise. We will work with you often. You may refer to yourself as someone that channels or receives direct communication from angels."
> —The White Angels

I have spent many early-morning hours in my meditation room communicating with angels. In the beginning, it took me a while to realize what was happening. Typically, I would awaken around 3:00 a.m. with a surge of energy in my solar plexus chakra. This was followed by a prompting to get up and meditate.

Prior to each session, I prepare my meditation room by lighting candles and incense. Then I sit on the floor in sukhasana (crossed legs) and begin with a prayer to clear the room—and my mind—from everything but love and light. It is from the deepest meditation that I find my connection to God. Once connected, I pray for guidance and understanding.

I understand the messages from the angels through a clear knowing; metaphysically this is called claircognizance. Claircognizance is one of the four metaphysical senses. The other three are clairvoyance (clear seeing), clairaudience (clear hearing), and clairsentience (clear feeling). When I communicate with angels, it is through claircognizance, and when I see angels, it is through clairvoyance. Sometimes these metaphysical senses are collectively referred to as a "sixth sense." Most people have a tendency toward one of these gifts, clairsentience being the most common (if you have ever walked into a room and felt a strange vibe, you were tapping into your clairsentient ability). Everyone possesses the ability to heighten their metaphysical senses simply by raising their vibration.

"Your heavenly parents would not send you to this earth without wishing to communicate with you. Many of you feel unworthy to commune with heaven and angels, believing it is left only for ascended masters, saints, and sages. All of you possess this ability. Communication is best received through a state of meditation. Meditation is the stilling of the mind so that one might hear the words of God.

"Communing with the Divine is not easily achieved, nor is it automatic. It takes much persistence and a pure desire from the heart. God hears the prayers of those that pray from the heart. When humankind cries out in need, answers from above are received because the heart is pure in that moment. Many prayers are left unheard because they are not sincere coming from the mind and not the heart.

"To fully communicate, one must pray, followed by silent meditation, for it is in stillness that one hears the voice of God. Take comfort and know this is your Divine birthright. Night and day, communicate with the above. Ask for God's blessings to be poured upon your head. There is no limit to the abundant blessings that await each of you, but you must ask. It is up to you, Divine child of the universe, to open the gates of communication with a pure heart, a strong desire, and a true belief.

"You are a Divine spark of creation. There is no

limit to the gifts and messages that await you. Do not fear that you know not how to reach God. Speak like a child with a pure heart and simple mind. Do not wait, begin today. Ask for help from the angels, and we will guide your way. You are loved."
— The White Angels

When guardian angels come to me on behalf of another, they usually appear as male or female. Knowing that angels are non-gender beings of light, I asked the White Angels about this. They explained to me that because we live in a physical dimension, angels sometimes show themselves in forms that we can relate to and understand from our physical perspective.

"What is more important is to feel our energy and listen to our guidance, believe we exist and ask for our help. Do not get distracted by the details. Focus on the grander scheme, which is our divine purpose, helping humankind progress and expand individually and collectively."
— The White Angels

One evening, after beginning a writing with the White Angels, I was told I could not continue. They explained that my vibration was too low for clear communication due to the alcohol I had at dinner. I stopped drinking alcohol during my time at the ashram, but once in a while I would have a small glass of wine with dinner. This particular night I literally had two sips of red wine, and it had apparently affected my vibration. Feeling a bit chastised, I realized I had to commit to this work 100 percent and nothing less. Later that week, the angels informed me I needed to give up my beloved coffee—no caffeine was the message. Keeping my vibration high would mean that I had to live clean and eat clean. No alcohol, no caffeine, and no meat. I was a vegetarian, so no meat was not a struggle. They taught me a very important lesson about keeping my vibration high.

The White Angels informed me that the messages I had been receiving in the early hours of the morning were to be shared for the benefit of others. **"This is your duty and your responsibility, it is what you were called forward to do. Share your knowledge and your light with the world. Do not hide our messages and your talents."** I had no idea how I was going to share these messages. Fear of rejection and chastisement kept me from moving forward. I was indeed hiding my talents under a bushel and kept the fact that I communicated with angels to a select few. Fear's paralyzing grip can keep us from achieving many of our dreams and creating the reality we want to live. It was clear that I had to move beyond my fear and learn this very difficult lesson.

"God is the master creator. He has created all things in the universe and beyond. Creativity is a gift from God to his children. Thought is the genesis of all creation. You are powerful creators capable of accomplishing great tasks beyond your comprehension. When you engage in the creative process, angels rejoice and stand by to assist. The very act of creating is Divine.

"Once something is created, the energy is eternal. Use holy and good intentions for your creations and create for the benefit of others. There are unlimited possibilities for using your gift of creation. It matters not what you create but the intention behind it. We say to you: go forth and create."

— The White Angels

Within a year, I was guided to write a book. I had never written a book, and other than a few articles I had published on fitness and yoga, I did not consider myself a "writer." My ego immediately began filling my head with doubts and fear of rejection. Fortunately, I did not give in, and with pen to paper, eventually the words started flowing. The White Angels informed me that it was crucial I keep my vibration high while writing this book for clear communication. They instructed me to meditate and pray before each writing session.

The universe works in mysterious ways. Once I set the intention to write, synchronicities began appearing. It was by divine intervention that I discovered my writer's paradise, and I have the angels to thank for orchestrating the arrangements. My husband, Joe, met two gentlemen, Marc and Nathan, who owned a charming place in the mountains of Idyllwild, California, aptly named the Quiet Creek Inn. Marc and Nathan invited Joe and I to visit, but Joe was too busy with work to get away. I took the opportunity, deciding it would be an ideal place to write with only birds, butterflies, and squirrels as my companions.

My cozy little cabin at the Quiet Creek Inn overlooked a babbling creek, from which I could hear the fresh mountain water rushing over rocks. I began each day with a long meditation. This set the vibration for the day and aligned me with God and the angels. Many days, I never got out of my pajamas and spent the entire day writing. Each night, I lit a fire in the fireplace and ended the day with another long meditation.

The energy in the cabin was magical. Some nights I was up all night receiving messages from the White Angels and did not sleep. I never knew what the topic would be until I began writing. Thoughts came as a constant flow of information downloaded into my mind. At times, I struggled to put into words the beautiful messages I received. I felt my vocabulary was limited, and the full meaning of these divine messages would be lost in translation. I did not have time to stop and contemplate the messages during the channeling session because of the speed at which they were given. I wrote the messages in a notebook, and in the morning, I transferred them onto the computer. Typing the message on the computer gave me time to reread the words from the night before and to contemplate the meaning. The experience was miraculous.

> "There are many messages from heaven that are beyond the scope of your understanding. The human vocabulary is too limited to express these concepts. The human mind, at its current capacity, cannot grasp the magnitude of the knowledge available. It is for this reason that we utilize the superconscious mind during your sleeping hours to communicate and educate you."
> — The White Angels

Marc and Nathan keep copies of the Bible, the Teaching of Buddha, the Bhagavad Gita, and Jing Si Aphorisms in the room for their guests to enjoy. Each book is unique and filled with universal truths and words of wisdom from which we can all learn. These truths resonate differently with all of us. The search for knowledge and wisdom is a personal one that we internalize on our journey through life. It is only through the heart that you discover the truth in all things. During my stay at the Quiet Creek Inn, I enjoyed reading a passage from each book at night before going to bed, hoping to extract a precious nugget of wisdom.

"The seeds of knowledge, once planted, grow the trees of wisdom. Knowledge illuminates ignorance, shinning a light upon that which is unreal and untrue. Ignorance is then burned in the fire of wisdom to be abolished forever more. Seek ye the angels of knowledge and wisdom. Ask for their blessings to be upon your head. Remove the veil of ignorance placed upon you, and know that you are a powerful child of God capable of great things. Search for knowledge of that which is true and good, and discern with wisdom the exactitude of that knowledge.

"The fruits of the tree of knowledge are hidden within. One must dive deep in the solitude and stillness of meditation to uncover them. Truth and knowledge do not come from the mind, but the heart. Do not be deceived by the cunning mind as it is governed by the ego. It is the heart that is the true navigator of all knowledge. Look to the heart and you will find wisdom in all things. God placed you here on earth to learn the truth of all things— to discover and discern for yourself as His Divine child.

"If you look to the world for answers, you will only be misled. Look up to the heavens for that which you seek, and you will find the answers. Listen for those answers in silent meditation and communion with God. Ask the angels of knowledge and wisdom to guide your thoughts. Ask the angels of knowledge and wisdom to obliterate ignorance from your life and those around you. Ask God and the angels to shine their light upon you and your earthly brothers and sisters. Seek and ye shall find the truth in all things now and forever more."

— The White Angels

Chapter 2
Archangels and Guardian Angels

JOHANNSON

"I am sent directly from God to guard and guide you. You are surrounded by hosts of angels."

"And I saw 7 angels who stand before God; and to them were given seven trumpets."
Revelations 2:8

Angels are given a wide range of responsibilities depending on their classification. Archangels are large, powerful angels with a specific purpose to fulfill. The word "archangel" means chief angel in Greek. These chief angels are overseers of other angels and have been referenced in sacred Christian, Jewish, and Islamic texts. Archangels are omnipresent, meaning they can be present everywhere at once.

There are hundreds of archangels; however, most people are familiar with four iconic archangels: Michael, Gabriel, Raphael, and Uriel. These are the most called upon of all of the Archangels. The first book of Enoch (an ancient Jewish text) gives this account of the seven main archangels as follows:

1. Uriel, one of the holy angels, who is over the world, turmoil, and terror.

2. Raphael, one of the holy angels, who is over the spirits of men.

3. Raguel, one of the holy angels, who takes vengeance on the world of the luminaries.

4. Michael, one of the holy angels, set over the virtues of mankind and over chaos.

5. Saraqael (Raziel), one of the holy angels, who is set over the spirits, who sin in the spirit.

6. Gabriel, one of the holy angels, who is over Paradise, the serpents, and the Cherubim.

7. Remiel (Jeremiel), one of the holy angels, whom God set over those who rise.

Archangel Uriel, whose name means "God is my light,"

is the archangel of peace both for us individually and for our global community. Uriel is God's illuminator, shedding light on all situations, places, people, and things. He is considered one of the "angels of presence," or angels that are allowed to enter the presence of God. "In all their affliction he was afflicted, and the angel of his presence saved them: in his love and in his pity, he redeemed them; and he bare them, and carried them all the days of old" (Isaiah 63:9).

It was Archangel Uriel who warned Noah of the imminent flood. Archangel Uriel illuminates our path and works with those whose life's purpose is to spread peace around the world. Archangel Uriel has a gentle and wise energy. I refer to him as the "wise old soul" of the archangels. You might not feel his presence like the other angels because he is so gentle and peaceful, but that does not mean he is not near.

Call upon Archangel Uriel to bring peace to you and your loved ones and peace to the world. Archangel Uriel's purpose is to "shine the light" on all things, so ask him to illuminate any project you have or invoke him anytime you need inspiration and information. I invoke his help when a local or global tragic event has taken place. I ask him to send light to the situation and light to all involved.

Archangel Raphael is the "patron of healers" whose name means "The shining one who heals." He is mentioned in the Book of Tobit (a book of scripture that is part of the Catholic and Orthodox biblical canon) for his help in healing Tobit's blindness. I work closely with Archangel Raphael and call upon him often in my work as a Reiki master.

Archangel Raphael is also the "patron of travelers."

Whenever I travel, I ask Archangel Raphael to ensure that I have a smooth and effortless trip. By doing so, I am guaranteed that my flight will be on time and my luggage will arrive at my intended destination. He is my angelic travel agent and GPS guidance system. I never travel without him!

You can call upon Archangel Raphael whenever you are sick or a loved one is ill. Ask for his help when you have a sick pet or an animal that needs healing (he will also help to retrieve a lost pet). If you are traveling, call upon Archangel Raphael to arrange a smooth and stress-free journey.

Archangel Raguel is the angel that watches over the behavior of the angels, guardian angels, and archangels. His name means "Friend of God." He is known as the "angel of friendship." Archangel Raguel brings peace and harmony to any situation and helps resolve conflicts and misunderstandings. Because of this, he is referred to as the "angel of justice and fairness." I consider Archangel Raguel to be the divine mediator.

Call upon Archangel Raguel when you need help with a friendship or legal matter. Ask him to bring peace and harmony to your relationships. Ask for his divine intervention with any conflicts and misunderstandings, and ask that he shine his light on truth.

Archangel Michael is the most familiar of all archangels. His name means "Who is as God." Archangel Michael is the most powerful of all of the archangels and is considered the "Protector of all evils" (he has been deemed the patron of police officers). It was Archangel Michael that led Joan of Arc into battle. His energy is very strong. Archangel Michael releases us from negative energy and empowers us with confidence and courage. His energy is so strong that I feel hot and flushed when he is around.

Call upon Archangel Michael when you need protection or when you feel afraid, as he helps cut the cords of fear that bind us and protects us from evil. Ask him to protect your family and pets and all that you love. Consider him your personal bodyguard from above! In addition to being our protector, he helps provide direction with our life path and works with Lightworkers, or spiritually-oriented people who believe they are here for a divine purpose to help humanity. Ask him to guide and direct your spiritual path and life purpose.

Archangel Saraqael is more commonly known today as Archangel Raziel. He is the angel chief over the thrones, guarding the secrets of the universe. It is no surprise then that his name means "Secret of God." Raziel is known as the "keeper of secrets" and the "angel of mysteries." It is said that Raziel wrote down these secrets and mysteries in *The Book of Raziel the Angel.* According to Hebrew legend, the book was given to Adam in the Garden of Eden by the hand of God. Raziel is the wizard of the archangels, helping us to better understand the esoteric and metaphysical world.

Call upon Archangel Raziel to help in understanding the laws of the universe and the divine principles upon which it was created. Ask for his help in developing your psychic abilities of clairvoyance, claircognizance, clairsentience, and clairaudience. Ask for his guidance if you have a desire to teach or write about spiritual subjects.

Archangel Gabriel is the messenger angel. Gabriel means "God is my strength" or "Hero of God." Archangel

Gabriel is referenced in the New Testament: "And the Angel answering said unto him, I am Gabriel, that stand in the presence of God; and am sent to speak unto thee, and to shew thee these glad tidings" (Luke 1:19). Some refer to Gabriel as a male, and yet others have seen her as a female. When I see Archangel Gabriel, I see a non-gender angel with equal female and male energy, though I will refer to her as she. The Persian poet Ruzbihan Baqli wrote, "I saw Gabriel, like a maiden, or like the moon amongst the stars. His hair was like a woman's, falling in long tresses... He is the most beautiful of angels..."

Archangel Gabriel works with artists, musicians, writers, actors, and anyone with a life purpose that involves communication. It was Archangel Gabriel that came to me with the message that I needed to write a book and now guides my writing. I have a small statue of Gabriel on my desk, and I invoke her each time I sit down to write. She lovingly presented a golden pen to me one night while I was writing. She explained that the pen symbolizes "writing golden words from the light."

Call upon Archangel Gabriel if you are writing a book, have a spiritual message to deliver to the world, or need help with a creative project. Invoke her help if you are beginning a career in the arts or communication.

Archangel Remiel is more commonly known today as Archangel Jeremiel, whose name means "Mercy of God." Jeremiel is known as the "angel of visions and dreams," and for this reason he is helpful in developing your clairvoyant skills. He is the archangel of life reviews here on earth, helping us to see the past, present, and future, and aligning to our true purpose here. In addition, Archangel Jeremiel helps newly departed souls with their life review once they have crossed over.

We do not need to wait to depart before asking Jeremiel's help in evaluating our life and taking inventory of where we are on our spiritual journey in this life. Call upon Archangel Jeremiel for help in seeking a new direction for your future. Ask him to help with dream interpretations. Ask for his help in developing clairvoyance, your psychic sight (located at the third eye), and seeing the bigger picture of your current life.

According to the third book of Enoch, the most powerful and greatest of all archangels is Metatron. The meaning of his name has not been defined, but he has been referred to in *The Book of Enoch* as "the Lesser YHWH," "the Prince of the Presence," and "Youth." The last name is likely due to the fact that Metatron is considered the newest and youngest archangel. The book describes the link between Enoch, the son of Jared (great-grandfather of Noah) and his transformation into an angel. Metatron confirms in *The Book of Enoch* that he is indeed Enoch when he says, "Because I am Enoch, the son of Jared... who was taken to heaven."

Metatron is unique in the respect that few archangels have had a human incarnation, with the exception of Archangel Sandalphon, who was said to be the prophet Elijah.

Archangel Metatron oversees our ascension process here on earth. Because he has had a physical incarnation, he is a bridge between heaven and earth, teaching us how to work with the angelic realm. Archangel Metatron oversees the flow of energy through the sacred geometry of Metatron's Cube. This sacred cube contains every shape that exists in the universe (known as the Platonic solids). Call upon Archangel Metatron and his healing cube to clear you of any negative energies.

Guardian angels, unlike archangels, are not omnipresent. Guardian angels are assigned to protect and guide a specific individual during their lifetime. We are each given a guardian angel at birth to be our constant companion. Some feel unworthy to have a guardian angel, but God does not discriminate. Regardless of our actions and behaviors we are all equally blessed with a guardian angel to watch over and guide us. Think of your guardian angel as a gift from God that will guide and direct you to complete your purpose on earth and fulfill your life's mission.

It has been my privilege to work with guardian angels on behalf of my clients. (I have included illustrations of some of these guardian angels at the beginning of each chapter with a name and a quote from these benevolent beings.) Every guardian angel is beautiful and unique. Some of the guardian angels I have seen appear young and attractive, while others are simply a bright light or flame. I was surprised to see many of the angels dressed in colorful clothing, holding objects, or wearing a wreath around their head. I started to see a pattern evolve around the color of the angel's clothing and the chakras they represent. This correlation proves helpful in assessing the emotional healing needed by my clients.

Every guardian angel provides me with a name. Most of these names are foreign to me, so following a session, I research the meaning on the Internet. I have often found that the name of the guardian angel relates to some aspect of my client. For example, one client's guardian angel introduced herself as Sarahi, which means princess in Hebrew. In the message, Sarahi told my client that she needed to discover her "inner princess." Another client, whose guardian angel's name is Philipa (meaning "lover of horses"), had been around horses all her adult life, and her livelihood was dependent upon them at one time.

Meeting my guardian angel was an event that changed my life. It happened early one morning around 3:00 a.m. Suddenly, I was awakened out of a deep sleep. I heard a still, small voice that whispered, "You must get up and go outside." I promptly ignored the voice and pulled the covers around my shoulders. My four-pound Chihuahua, Harry, sensing my restlessness, snuggled in closer to me. *Why would I leave my cozy warm bed to go stand outside in the cold?* I heard the voice again, and this time it was loud and clear: "Go outside." Against my better judgment, I slipped out of bed, trying not to disturb my husband and our two dogs, all sound asleep. Slowly and still half asleep, I made my way to the backyard, wondering if maybe I was going crazy!

Standing outside and looking up at the stars was magic. The beautiful full moon illuminated the backyard like a spotlight. The cool, damp grass felt surprisingly refreshing on my bare feet, and the gentle night breeze blew through my robe. There was an eerie quiet that penetrated the air as I stood all alone in the night. I could hear a barn owl, which seemed to be hooting from a nearby cypress tree. There I was, all alone with this massive universe staring down at me. I felt small, like a child gazing out into space in wonder and in awe.

Suddenly, I heard the still, small voice again. Tingles ran up and down my spine and the name Johannson popped into my head. *How strange,* I thought to myself, *who is Johannson?*

I looked to the stars for an answer, and in the stillness of the night, the answer came to me. Johannson is my guardian angel. It was like a confirmation from the heavens, a deep knowing in my soul. My body tingled as unconditional love penetrated my very being, and I felt at peace with all. I could feel Johannson's presence, and I knew he was there with me in the garden. A thousand questions began running through my head. *Why is he my guardian angel? Has he always been with me? What does he look like? Is this just my imagination or is this real?*

Dawn was beginning to break, and Mother Nature was waking up. I suddenly felt exhausted and needed to go back to bed. Joe, my husband, was just getting up to feed the dogs.

"What are you doing up so early?" he asked.

"You would not believe me if I told you," I replied. I went back into bed and crawled under the covers, knowing my life would never be the same.

I began communicating with Johannson daily. I talked to him like he was my new best friend, sharing my thoughts and feelings. It was comforting to know that I was not alone. Someone was there to watch over me and protect me.

Another responsibility of our guardian angels is protection. Our guardian angels protect us from danger if it is not our time to die. If we only knew how much divine help surrounds us, we would never fear or worry. "For he will command his angels concerning you to guard you in all your ways" (Psalms 91:11). Because of the universal law of "free will," our guardian angel can only help us if we ask. The only exception to this law is when we are in danger and it is not our time to leave our physical body.

The Internet is full of accounts and stories of guardian angels coming to the rescue of children, adults, and animals. Think back to a time in your life that you might have been rescued in the face of danger. Perhaps someone in your family has a story like this to tell. It is often in times of crisis that we are aware of the angels around us, but we do not need to wait until tragedy strikes to call upon our guardian angels for help. Invoking the help of your guardian angel can be as simple as thinking, "Guardian angel, help me now." When you ask from your heart, the angels respond immediately for your greatest and highest good. Remember to always thank your angels for the service they render on your behalf.

My guardian angel stepped in to save my life on four separate occasions. The first time my life was spared, I was too young to remember, so I rely on my parents' recollection. At the time, Mom and Dad were living in Columbus, Ohio. Dad was a young science student, getting a PhD in microbiology at the Ohio State University. They lived on a shoestring budget in a small one-bedroom apartment that Mom cleverly furnished with items from a local thrift store. Mom was a master seamstress and could transform any room with a bolt of fabric and a gallon of paint.

One morning, Mom was busy cleaning the apartment and doing her best to keep an eye on me. I was walking at the time and getting into everything. Mom gathered the cleaning supplies she stored under the kitchen sink and went to work. I must have seen her get into the cupboard and, like any other toddler, I became curious. In addition to holding cleaning supplies, this cupboard was also where the Drano was kept. Drano came in a box filled with little crystalline rocks that, when poured down the sink, unclogged the drain. A little box of crystals must have looked like candy to me, and I proceeded to eat three of them. Hearing my screams, Mom rushed into the kitchen to see the box beside me and blisters forming all over my lips.

The next few moments were a blur for Mom, but she remembered calling for an ambulance and watching in hysteria as her baby was taken to the hospital. Miraculously, the crystals did not burn a hole in my esophagus or stomach. The doctor said it was a miracle I survived, and he told Mom that if she had waited a minute longer to call the hospital, my injuries would have been fatal. My guardian angel intervened that day, as it was not yet my time to die.

I was in high school the second time my life was spared. It was a sunny spring afternoon and my girlfriend Kim was driving us home from school in her bright yellow Ford Pinto station wagon we nicknamed Bernie Lemon. Bernie Lemon had nylon seatbelts with a heavy silver buckle that felt like I was wearing some kind of armor around my waist. The seatbelts were uncomfortable and inconvenient, so I didn't use them.

Kim and I loved music, and we spent countless hours after school listening to David Bowie and Elton John albums on her record player. On our way to Kim's house that day, our favorite new song came on the radio. The lyrics were racy and the tune upbeat, and we were singing, "Do a little dance, make a little love, get down tonight," at the top of our lungs, oblivious to the world outside. This might explain why Kim did not see the black Cadillac coming toward us at fifty miles an hour. While stopped at a red light, she suddenly decided to turn left, and the Cadillac hit the passenger's side of the vehicle where I was sitting. One minute I was singing, and the next I was lying unconscious on the pavement with blood pouring from my head.

The car behind us stopped to help. The driver was a doctor and called immediately for an ambulance, then proceeded to take care of me while we waited. A school bus passed by and many students saw me lying in a pool of blood and assumed the worst. The next day, rumors circulated around school that I had died in a horrible automobile accident, which fortunately was not the case. I had a concussion and a large gash in my head that took sixty stitches, but my life was saved. I don't believe it was mere coincidence that the driver in the car behind us happened to be a doctor; in fact, I believe he was divine intervention. I am not sure if I ever thanked him, but he saved my life that day, with a little help from Johannson.

The third time Johannson intervened, I was living in Los Angeles with my best friend, Dottye. Dottye was dating a young, good-looking country music artist at the time. His first album was out, and he was on his way to becoming a national heartthrob. One night he invited us to see him play at a local club in Hollywood called the Anti Club. The Anti Club was in a rough neighborhood on Melrose Avenue, close to the 101 Freeway.

When we got to the club, the parking lot was full, so we

decided to park Dottye's two-toned blue-and-silver Subaru down the street a few blocks away. It was almost 11 p.m., which meant we were fashionably late, but the night was still young. Walking toward the club, we could see a white Cadillac driving suspiciously slow. Upon taking a closer look, I saw the car was a lowrider and all of the windows were blacked out. Dottye turned to me and said, "Keep your eyes open, Ani. I have a bad feeling."

We crossed the street and had one more block to go, but before she could even finish her sentence, the Cadillac pulled around the corner and stopped. Three men got out of the car, screaming obscenities at us and shouting, "Stop, we have a gun."

One never knows what they will do when confronted with a life-or-death situation. Will I scream? Will I freeze? Will I cry? That moment was like a freeze frame, a motionless image that stopped for a split second and then resumed in full chaos. All I remember in that instant was the flash of the pearl handle on the gun, two men getting out of the backseat, and the red quilted interior of the car.

There was no time to think, and I was guided to run down the center of the busy Melrose Avenue. It was either get hit by a car or get thrown into the car with those men, and I chose the first option. I ran like hell and didn't look back. I flew into the Anti Club screaming and crying, not making much sense in my hysteria. The owner of the club heard the chaos and came to help. Surrounded with an army of friends and a few security guards from the club, I went back to the scene to find Dottye. However, there was no sign of Dottye and no sign of the white Cadillac.

My heart was in my throat as I considered the possibilities. *This can't be happening,* I told myself. I continued frantically calling her name when she suddenly appeared out of the bushes she was hiding in. Instinctively, we ran in the opposite direction when we saw the car—Dottye hiding in bushes while I ran down the center of a busy street. Reunited, we grabbed each other, shaking and crying, while the security guards breathed a sigh of relief. By divine intervention, the Cadillac was nowhere to be found, and we were both safe.

Looking back on that night, I often wondered how I made it to the club. Having been faced with outrunning those men in my five-inch stilettos, the odds were clearly stacked against me. I remember turning to run, but then my mind draws a blank and everything becomes a blur. My guardian angel later revealed to me that he carried me to safety that night. I literally flew into the Anti Club because my feet never touched the ground.

It was a sizzling hot summer day in Los Angeles when my life was spared a fourth time. The annual Los Angeles street fair was going on downtown, and my friends and I decided to attend. We spent the afternoon listening to our favorite bands, drinking beer, and people watching. The beers finally caught up with me, and I had to use the bathroom. Unfortunately, the only option was to stand in the long line for the dreaded porta-potty, but I was desperate.

Waiting impatiently beside me was my boyfriend, Gregory. Gregory was from Manchester, England, and knew a thing or two about life. His dashing good looks, English accent, and street smarts were a provocative combination.

The line seemed endless, and with my legs now crossed, a young woman cut in front of me. She stood there defiantly staring me down with her dark, piercing eyes and excessive black eyeliner. Immediately, I yelled a few obscenities at her and told her to move to the back of the line. A shoving match began, and out of nowhere her boyfriend showed up wearing the colors of one of the local LA gangs.

Gregory watched as her boyfriend pulled a silver switch-blade out of his pocket, ready to take care of the situation. Before I knew what was happening, Gregory grabbed my arm and we were running as fast as our legs could carry us.

"Bloody hell, woman, were you trying to get yourself killed?" he yelled in his angry but always charming English accent. I had no intention of such a thing, and neither did Johannson.

Chapter 3

Angels in My Childhood

LILITH

*"You are a valiant soul. Mother Mary is always near.
You are greatly loved."*

**"See that you do not despise one of these little ones.
For I tell you that their angels in heaven always see
the face of my Father in heaven."
—Matthew 18:10**

I learned about angels early in life. I grew up in a very
religious family, and church was a central part of my child-

hood. My parents came from a very long lineage of Mormons, tracing their ancestry back to the pioneers crossing the plains. We have books on our Mormon genealogy with stories describing the trials and tribulations they encountered settling the southeastern tip of Utah. One of my favorite stories told by my grandmother was when Butch Cassidy and the Sundance Kid spent the night in her great grandparents' attic while passing through on their way to Moab, Utah. Butch apparently snuck out of the house disguised as a woman to make a clean getaway. They spoke highly of Butch Cassidy and said he was a real gentleman. (Rumor had it that he was a Mormon.)

As a typical Mormon family, we attended church for three hours on Sunday. We were taught at an early age about God and Jesus and the angels (a golden statue of Angel Moroni sits atop each of the Mormon temples). One of our traditions as a Mormon family was kneeling together in family prayer each night. My little brother Stan's prayers usually included the next toy he had his eye on, and I was never sure if he was talking to God or Santa.

Mom and Dad explained to us that God lived somewhere in a place far away called Heaven. I pictured Heaven full of beautiful flowers, rainbows of every color, fluffy white clouds, and angels playing harps. I imagined unlimited amounts of ice cream and candy and animals of every size, shape, and color roaming together peacefully. In my young, impressionable mind, Heaven was where God sat on His golden throne, watching over all of us from above.

As I got older, my impression of Heaven changed. "Heaven is the three degrees of glory," Dad would explain. "The

Celestial, Telestial, and Terrestrial." Hell, on the other hand, was a place called Purgatory, and no one wanted to go there. Our goal as Mormons was to make it to the celestial kingdom, the highest kingdom where God resides. It is only attainable if you are a member of good standing in the eyes of the church. I remember as a young girl thinking that most of my friends would not make it to the celestial kingdom because they were not Mormon. This caused me great concern and grief. I wanted to be where all of my friends were and didn't like the idea of segregation. I experienced enough segregation as a child living in North Carolina.

Mom and Dad moved us to Durham, North Carolina, during a time of racial conflict. It was the early 1960s and Dad was teaching at Duke University. Durham was a city divided between black and white, and we felt the effects as small children. The three-story brick elementary school I attended was segregated with an unspoken "white children only" rule. Our housekeeper, Margaret, came to our home on the bus each day from the other side of town. Margaret wore a floral print housecoat with a white apron tied around her extra-large waist. Her hands were as big as a man's, yet her touch was soft and gentle, just like her voice. Margaret would not eat at our table. "No, it ain't right for me to eat with y'all," she would say upon my pleading.

April 1968 proved to be a pivotal turn for the civil rights movement. Dr. Martin Luther King Jr. was shot and killed on April 4 of that year, and riots broke out all around the country. Downtown Durham was ablaze with fires that we could see from our home on North Gregson Street. Our neighbor's furniture store was a casualty of these fires. Peeking through closed curtains, my brothers and I would watch the National Guard march down our street. "Get away from that window," Mom would say. She was trying hard to hide her own fears of the chaos that surrounded us.

At night, a mandatory curfew was put into place, and the streets looked like a ghost town. We had to be in our homes by 6:00 p.m. every evening. Dad listened to Walter Cronkite on the evening news to keep abreast of the activities across the country. One night, while listening to the news, the doorbell rang. Four police officers standing in uniform asked Dad if they could have access to our driveway that evening, as we were located on one of the main streets. Our five-bedroom white colonial home sat on top of a hill with a long driveway that could accommodate multiple cars.

I distinctly remember the flashing red lights on the police cars parked in our driveway. I could see the officers in uniform with their intimidating weapons strapped to their hips. I could hear the sounds of their voices and the dispatch officers on their walkie-talkies. I didn't understand what was happening or why. That night during our family prayers, Mom and Dad asked God to watch over us and keep us safe. Little did they know that Archangel Michael was there protecting the police officers and our home, and we were being watched over from above.

The civil unrest proved to be a turning point in my parent's decision to move us to California. Dad had an opportunity to start his own company, and my parents were ready to leave the South and its troubles behind. Southern California had its own problems at the time with the media frenzy around the Manson murders. *Why were we moving to a place where hippies slaughtered pregnant women? Would Charles*

Manson come and get us? My nine-year-old imagination ran wild and many nightmares followed. It wasn't until our first trip to Disneyland that I began to see the benefits of living in Southern California. I still had a heavy southern accent and missed hushpuppies and grits, but Mickey and Minnie were magical, and Disneyland was, after all, "the happiest place on earth."

Another happy place for me as a child was a small town called Ferron. Ferron, located in Emery County, Utah, had a population of 2,000. It was the town Mom and Dad grew up in, and as a result, I was related to most of the town in some way or another. Our family went to Ferron two or three times a year to visit our grandparents and relatives. We never missed the beginning of deer-hunting season every October. It was a big event in Ferron, and all of my relatives participated. The men put on bright orange vests and hats to keep them safe and spent the entire week at the cabin hunting deer.

During the hunt, my brothers and I stayed in town with all of the women. There was always a homemade pie baking in Grandma's oven or a fresh lime soda at the soda fountain to keep us occupied. Grandma worked at the soda fountain (which was owned by Uncle Darrell, her brother-in-law), and it was always a treat to go sit on the old-fashioned red stools and watch as Grandma created a chocolate malt or hot-fudge sundae for us. When the hunt was finally over, we headed back to California with a cooler full of venison to last for the year. My brothers and I often complained to Mom that we wanted to eat beef like everyone else and felt very deprived. As a strict vegetarian, I no longer eat meat, but the memories of those days are priceless.

One Christmas we packed up the family Vista Cruiser and headed to Ferron to visit the grandparents. Little did we know that along with all the suitcases and presents we had a car full of angels with us. This was in the early 70s when seatbelt laws were a thing of the future, so Dad would make a big bed in the back with pillows and blankets for us to lay on. Mom packed a cooler full of sandwiches and yummy snacks for the ride so that we wouldn't have to stop on our twelve-hour drive.

Pepe, our family dog (a cockapoo), always accompanied us on our family road trips. He would snuggle in beside one of us and sleep most of the trip unnoticed (until he passed gas!). Despite the cooler full of goodies, Dad stopped about every four hours for a treat. It irritated Mom, but it was what made the trip so special for us kids. The last stop of the day we all jumped out of the car to stretch our legs and get a final snack while Dad fueled up the car. Bulls-Eyes were my favorite penny candy. I loved the chewy caramel and creamy center, but occasionally I would get a crunchy one that had been sitting on the shelf too long.

After a gas and bathroom break, we piled back into the station wagon and headed off to Grandma's house. I knew once I saw the big oak tree and smelled cow manure that we were close. After many hours of asking the age-old question, "Are we there yet?" we reached the final destination. Grandma's red brick A-frame house was covered in climbing roses and looked like it belonged somewhere in the Cotswolds. Grandma was standing at the door waiting for us while one by one we fled the car and ran to her arms for hugs and kisses.

With all of the excitement, no one noticed that we were missing one small passenger: Pepe! Pepe was still at the gas station, so Dad quickly hurried off to retrieve him. Arriving at the station, Dad found Pepe sitting in the dark all alone right where we left him. He was cold and frightened, but he hadn't moved a foot. Finally, after four long hours, Dad returned with Pepe and it was a family reunion filled with laughter and wet doggy kisses. Because of the angels, we were reunited with our beloved family pet that Christmas.

Thanks to loving parents, I was given a solid foundation in God, and I knew I was never alone. When I became a mother, I relied upon my upbringing to guide my parental decisions. My children are a gift from God and the biggest blessings in my life; however, it was not an easy task bringing up two daughters as a single mother. God was my co-parent and I spent many nights on my knees in Divine communication searching for answers. Later when I began writing with the White Angels, they delivered this message on parenting. I only wish I had had it twenty years ago when I was a young mother.

> "Parenting is an agreement made between the child and parents prior to coming into this incarnation. It is a mutual agreement from all parties involved, each choosing the other in the designated roles. These roles are determined for various reasons but mainly to help each other grow and progress on their journey back to the Divine. Nothing is not known prior to coming down into the physical experience. This does not take into consideration that once born, the veil is closed so all previous knowledge of these agreements is forgotten.

> "The trials of family life are many on this planet.

Many times there is discord between family members. The lessons to be learned in these family communities are valuable, the most important being unconditional love, yet this is the most difficult. Children are not the property of the parents to control from their limited perspective. They are children of the Divine that are given into custody to the parent to love and guide to adulthood. Many parents are small in their thinking and have not expanded their awareness to include this knowledge.

"A child is a priceless gift from God to each parent and should be respected as such. Each child is born with their own individual personality, their own life purpose and their own karma. Once the parent understands this, the desire to mold the child's destiny to meet the parent's agenda is no longer attempted. God is the ultimate parent represented as the Divine mother and Divine father. We are all Divine children who must learn to love each other and get along."
— The White Angels

Nothing in creation is random. This is true for each of us and the lives we are living. Prior to coming to Earth, we decide our life purpose, the family we are born into, and the lessons we need to learn based on our karma. We do not make these decisions alone, but with those souls that lovingly agree to interact with us in this lifetime for our growth and expansion. We make contracts with these individuals for the greatest and highest good of our spiritual development. These contracts can be extremely challenging to experience on this earthly plane. Think of the individuals you have had the most difficulty with—they could be a family member, with a colleague, or an ex-partner. These relationships are here to teach you something. They are your greatest lessons.

I was taught in my childhood to love and respect my parents and siblings. It was a valuable lesson given by two loving parents that embody the Divine mother and father aspect. That love and respect continues as my siblings and I have grown into adults with children of our own. I am no longer a Mormon, but I am forever grateful for the foundation in God my parents established in our home.

Chapter 4

The City of Angels

MALIK

"Forgive yourself by releasing and letting go.
Love yourself, and love others."

"I feel that there is an angel inside me whom I am
constantly shocking."
—Jean Cocteau

My friend Sonia recently wrote a book titled *Losing the Plot in LA*. In her book, she chronicles the life of a young twenty-year-old girl and the crazy situations she gets herself into. Although the book is not about me, the title of the book summarizes my years living in Los Angeles. The book is set in 1984, which ironically was the same time period I was losing the plot there. It was an interesting time in LA—cocaine and big hair were in fashion, and AIDS was not yet on the radar.

Angels were also missing from my radar during this period of time in my life. Caught up in the seduction of the 80s, I was too preoccupied with the drama of life to seek after its deeper meaning. It would take many years before I would hear the whispers of my angels calling me.

After attending Brigham Young University, I returned home to San Diego. It was a difficult break-up that set in motion my move to Los Angeles. Steven was a heartbreaker, eight years my senior, and my boss at the time. I knew better than to date my boss—all of the statistics pointed toward disaster—but he was incredibly good-looking and drove a Ferrari, so I couldn't resist. It was an eighteen-year-old aerobics instructor that finally came between us. Replaced by a younger woman, I was completely crushed and heartbroken.

Ironically, my best friend at the time, Dottye, found herself in a similar situation. Dottye had recently moved to San Diego from Atlanta, Georgia, and was living with her brother, Barry. Barry played baseball for the Padres, so she decided to pay him a visit and ended up staying. Dottye was a tall, gorgeous blonde with a heavy southern accent that she used to her full advantage. God blessed her with a body most women can only dream of.

One day after a game of tennis, Dottye's fiancé turned to her and said, "I don't want to marry a tennis wife." He explained that he wanted someone with more ambition and drive, a businesswoman, and he didn't see that potential in her. What he didn't know then was that one day Dottye would own her own company and become an extremely successful entrepreneur.

Dottye and I decided to pack up our things and move to Los Angeles. Dottye dreamed of being a professional model, and I had been offered a dance scholarship with Joe Tremaine, the hottest choreographer in the country. So off we went to the "City of Angels," Los Angeles, California, with two broken hearts and stars in our eyes.

Los Angeles was quite a departure for the two of us. Leaving the comforts of a full-time job in San Diego and furnished apartment on the beach did not prepare me for the lifestyle of a starving artist. Our first apartment was a one bedroom in a cockroach-infested duplex located in North Hollywood. It didn't take Dottye long to find a job, and within a few weeks she was working as a wardrobe assistant for a large television studio.

A professional dancer had three choices in those days: you could go to New York and dance on Broadway, go to Las Vegas and dance topless in a variety show, or you could go to Los Angeles and dance in music videos and industrials. Dancers and choreographers did not have agents in the early 80s, so we relied on the *Variety*, a weekly, local trade magazine for the entertainment industry. *Variety* was my Bible. I couldn't wait to get my hands on it and see what auditions were posted for the week.

One of my first auditions was a music video for a very famous rock star. The posting in the Variety stated that a minimum of five years' dance experience was required, along with a bathing suit and high heels for the audition. The music video was to be filmed at Venice Beach. With my résumé in hand, I anxiously headed for the studio.

Standing in line with five hundred beautiful blonde-haired, blue-eyed dancers was ego deflating. In most dance auditions, the choreographer teaches a routine, the dancers then perform the routine, and the elimination process begins. This audition was different. One by one, we waited for our name to be called and then we were ushered into an office. After hours of waiting in line, my name was finally called. With butterflies in my stomach, I entered a room to find the famous rock star sitting behind a very large desk. He invited me in and, with my résumé in his hand, proceeded to ask me some questions.

Where am I going to dance? my inner voice panicked. There was not enough room in his office to do a single pirouette. He then politely asked me to stand on top of his desk with only my bathing suit and high heels on. *WTF? He must be kidding,* I thought to myself. My knees began to tremble as I noticed a small stepping stool strategically placed in front of the desk. I placed one foot in front of the other and climbed on top of his desk until I was hovering above him.

"Please turn around and face the door," he requested politely. My back end was now facing him and I could feel the heat of his gaze. After a few minutes he said, "Okay, thank you, that will be all," and then he dismissed me.

An awkward pause filled the air before I realized that the audition was now over, and he wanted me off of his desk. I carefully placed one foot on the stool and then the other as I climbed down. My high-heeled character shoe slipped on the last step, and I came crashing down onto the floor, legs flailing in the air. Needless to say, I did not get the part. I can only imagine the roar of laughter that followed after I closed the door behind me.

Dottye and I traded the cockroach-infested apartment in North Hollywood for a tiny studio apartment in Marina Del Rey with an ocean view. It was pint-size, but we spent most of our time outside on the balcony watching our famous neighbors come and go. One day while sunning ourselves on our deck, we discussed how fun it would be to take a trip to Europe. I had dreamed of traveling abroad, but it seemed out of reach considering our financial status.

Spring fever kicked in, and logic went out the door. We were poor as church mice, but we didn't let that deter our plans. Dottye and I decided to fund the trip by selling her beloved Subaru. With no agenda, we stuffed two backpacks full of clothes, and headed to LAX with one-way tickets to London in our hot little hands. Neither of us was aware at the time that our guardian angels would be carefully watching over us on the trip, keeping us out of trouble.

The flight to London was long, but I couldn't sleep because I was so excited. We found lodging on our first night in London at the Luna House Hotel. It was a cozy little youth hostel on Kings Road that looked like a replica of the Haunted Mansion at Disneyland. Staying in youth hostels was the cheap way to see Europe, our travel book stated, and cheap was our mantra. After checking in at the front desk, we made our way up the creaky staircase to our assigned room. The sound of heavy rain and wind howled through the hallway, adding to the ambience.

When we opened the door to our room, we were surprised to see a couple of Scottish blokes sitting on one of the two bunk beds. The front desk had failed to mention it was coed accommodations, and Dottye and I were mortified. Fear crept in as we assessed their black Mohawks, tartan plaid pants, and torn leather jackets.

"Hallow, ladeze," one said with a thick Scottish accent. I noticed safety pins pierced through his earlobes, which contributed to his punk look. Despite (or perhaps because of) their appearance, it didn't take long before the two of them had us laughing hysterically at their irreverent humor. They invited us to join them for a night of clubbing on Kings Road. Setting aside any apprehensions, we agreed and headed out for our first night in London Town.

Kings Road was notorious in the 1970s and 80s as a center of punk culture. Our Scottish friends escorted us to one punk club after another as the music of The Sex Pistols and The Clash filled the air. The clubs were packed to capacity as pints of stout were consumed in excess. Video screens played the latest punk videos while girls dressed in torn fishnet tights, army boots, and fetish-wear danced to the music of The Clash and The Sex Pistols. Dottye and I stood out like sore thumbs with our white and pink Victoria Secret sweat suits amid the crowds of gothic youth. Our first night in London was one we would always remember.

After a week in rainy London, we decided it was time to explore sunnier spots in Europe. Soon we were country hopping, thanks to our Eurail passes, through Italy, France, Greece, Germany, Austria, Belgium, Denmark, Luxembourg, and Switzerland. The Berlin Wall had not yet fallen, so

Eastern Europe was off-limits to us at that time, but we had plenty of other options just one train ride away. We were two girls with no plan.

"Where do you want to go tomorrow?" Dottye would ask, and with that I would close my eyes and point on the map.

Leaving London, our next destination was Italy. Venice was magical. Saint Mark's Square, or Piazza San Marco, was the center of activity. We spent lazy afternoons on the square people watching while sipping espresso at outdoor cafés. The youth hostel we stayed at was conveniently located on one of the canals, and at night we could hear gondoliers serenading their passengers just outside our window. St. Mark's Basilica (Basilica di San Marco) was the most famous of all the churches in the city. The Gothic basilica is a beautiful representation of Italo-Byzantine architecture. The opulent golden interior with its gilded mosaics was breathtaking, but after five glorious days in Venice we decided it was time to move on.

Florence, or Firenze as it is known by the locals, is the capital of Tuscany. Unlike Venice, Florence is surrounded by vine-clad hills and idyllic gardens. Dottye and I didn't know where to begin with so many churches, palaces, museums, and monuments to explore. Walking the steps to the Piazzale Michelangelo at sunset provided a breathtaking view of the city only rivaled by the view from the top of the Duomo. The food in Florence is a spiritual experience. Even the pasta diablo (called "devil pasta" because of the heat) was heavenly! Our workout clothes were getting a little tight as we ate our way through Tuscany one gnocchi at a time.

Greece was next. To get to Greece, we took the train from

Florence to a city called Brindisi at the tip of Italy. From there, we would take the ferry over to Athens. Boarding the late train, we found our way to an empty car with the hope of catching up on some sleep. Soon we were both sound asleep and oblivious to the world. About halfway to Brindisi, we picked up an unwanted passenger. An Italian man snuck into our cab with ill intentions. He stood a little over five feet tall, pushing two hundred pounds. Someone (my guardian angel) told me to wake up, and I opened my eyes in time to see him drop his drawers.

I screamed Dottye's name and immediately she woke to see the intruder with his pants down. "*Cattivo, cattivo!*" she yelled at the top of her lungs. (She thought she was saying "You are the devil" but later we found out it means "bad one" in Italian.) Nevertheless, he got the message and made a mad dash out of the cabin holding his pants up with his hand! I'm not sure to this day what he hoped to accomplish, but he was certainly taking on more than he bargained for. We were too busy laughing to worry about chasing the short, round little man. Once we reached Brindisi, we saw him leave the train with his wife and children looking at us sheepishly like nothing had ever happened.

After Greece, Dottye and I traveled to Switzerland and France, stopping in picturesque villages and towns along the way. We stopped in Belgium and stayed in the beautiful port city of Brussels. The city was buzzing with excitement as they prepared for the European Cup Final between Italy and Liverpool. The streets were filled with Italians and English fans gearing up for the big game. Dottye and I loved people watching while sitting outside at a local café, indulging in mussels and frites. At night, the bars were full to capacity and alcohol was a catalyst for overzealous fans. The night before the game, the streets were crowded and fights broke out as tension mounted.

On the day of the event, I had an uneasy feeling that we needed to get out of town. I pointed to the map and we were off to Denmark on the first train out. Later, we heard reports of the "Heysel Stadium disaster." Fans standing near a retaining wall in the soccer stadium were crushed, killing thirty-nine people and injuring 600. Riots broke out in the city, and it was pure chaos. The disaster was described as the darkest hour in the history of the Union of European Football Association (UEFA). Thanks to our angels, we were far away and safe.

Two American girls backpacking through Europe was quite a spectacle. We were both big fans of the fitness explosion going on in the states, so we decided to take advantage of it on our travels. Each day we dressed in our workout shorts and tops with tennis shoes and weights strapped around our ankles. We were determined to stay in shape while in Europe, but the baguettes and pastries were winning out. In France, we were tempted with buttery croissants and crepes. In Denmark, we feasted on the Danish pastries, while in Switzerland we indulged in melt-in-your mouth Swiss chocolate. We tried every flavor of gelato in Italy, and did I leave out the sticky toffee pudding in England? (My favorite!)

Dottye and I had just polished off two large servings of apple strudel—Germany's most famous pastry—which we washed down with large German beers, and we felt stuffed and bloated. It was time to offset our indulgent snack with some exercise. Walking through the streets of Munich, with our ankle weights strapped tight, we spotted an extremely good-looking young man. He made his way over to us and asked if we were German aerobics instructors. *Nein!* we replied. We had a great laugh, and he introduced himself as Christian. He told us he was an actor and model working in Germany for the summer but home was Marina Del Rey.

Christian was one of many Americans we met on our travels. Many of them were young adults backpacking their way around Europe just like us. Spending the afternoon with Christian made me homesick for Los Angeles, and it occurred to me that I was ready to go back. Dottye agreed. After two and a half months in Europe, we were out of money and out of steam. The adventure had run its course, and we were pining for the United States. I wanted a proper American cheeseburger with curly fries and a Diet Coke. I wanted to see my family again, and I couldn't wait to sleep in my own bed. No more youth hostels or trains.

We booked a flight from Frankfurt, Germany, to Los Angeles, California. We arrived at the Frankfurt airport early with our backpacks now full of dirty clothes and souvenirs. When we arrived, the airport was in utter chaos. As smoke and sirens filled the air, it looked like the set on an action movie. Someone had planted a bomb in the trashcan at one of the departure lounges, which killed three people and wounded thirty-two. The airport was closed, and we were stranded.

This tragic situation augmented the desperate, homesick feeling that had been gnawing at my stomach. Dottye and I sat on a street corner, feeling hopeless and helpless without a plan B. The thought occurred to me that we had no place to stay for the evening and we were out of money. How would we eat and pay for shelter? I started sobbing; it was all too much to take in.

"We need a miracle," I said, and I began to pray to God for help. Not allowing me time to lament the situation, Dottye pulled me up by my backpack and forced me to my feet.

"Come on," she said. "Let's find a travel agency to get us out of here." (Unfortunately, we had no access to cell phones or Internet in those days.)

Wolfgang was the owner of the nearest travel agency. He heard about the bomb and could see the desperation on our faces when we walked into his office. Wolfgang had a kind face, slightly graying hair, and appeared to be in his mid-fifties. Fortunately, he spoke English and listened patiently as we explained our dilemma. Wolfgang informed us that he owned a hotel nearby and offered to put us up free for the night until the airport reopened. We couldn't believe our good fortune. We were tired, hungry, and still in shock from an unbelievable day, and this was a gift from God, an answer to my prayer.

Wolfgang called for a car to take us to his hotel. It was late when the white stretch limousine pulled up to the travel agency. As I climbed into the limousine and saw the white leather interior, I felt like Cinderella getting into her carriage.

"Get a good night sleep, girls, and we will work on your flight in the morning when the airport reopens," Wolfgang said in his heavy German accent. With a wave goodbye, we were off. The driver made his way deep into the Black Forest as we continued down the Autobahn Highway. "Where are we?" Dottye whispered in my ear. I had no clue, but I was too tired and hungry to worry about it.

The hotel was a scene out of Las Vegas. Lit up with neon lights, it sparkled like a jewel in the forest.

"Good evening, ladies. I have been expecting you," said the desk clerk. She looked like a quintessential grandmother, dressed in a floral smock with her gray hair pulled back in a bun. "Wolfgang tells me you are from California, so I am putting you in the San Francisco Suite tonight," she continued. Elsa escorted us to our room and informed us that dinner would be served downstairs in an hour. Our room was covered with a large, painted mural of San Francisco stretched across all four walls. The Golden Gate Bridge loomed over the fluffy white bed that beckoned to me. Pure exhaustion permeated every cell of my body.

"I'm starvin'!" Dottye squealed in delight as she jumped on the bed. After a gloriously long shower, I was ready for a hot meal and a good night's sleep.

The dining room was dark and empty, and in the center of the room was a large stage. Round tables were stationed in front of the stage with red leather booths at the perimeter of the room. We seated ourselves at a table directly in front of the stage, and we were guessing that the night's entertainment might be a burlesque show or comedy act. A young woman took our order, and I was pleased to see the hamburger and fries that I had fantasized about earlier in the day were on the menu. Dottye ordered the bratwurst and potatoes and we ordered two German beers to wash it all down.

Completely focused on inhaling our food, we were oblivious to the activities taking place on stage. The curtain had come up and to our shock we were sitting front and center to a live sex show. Mortified, Dottye looked down at her empty plate and immediately lit a cigarette. Curiosity got the best of me so I watched as men and women did things to each other I had never heard of. I was happy the room was dark because I knew my face was completely red. Although she was afraid to look up, Dottye wanted a play-by-play narration. "What are they doing now, Ani?" she asked.

After the curiosity had worn off, I felt uncomfortable and decided it was time to exit the scene. The fatigue of the day had set in, and I couldn't wait to get into the fluffy white bed waiting for me in the San Francisco Suite.

The next morning Elsa greeted us with her sweet, grandmother-like smile, with no mention of the sex show from the night before. Instead, she asked if we would like to see her zoo after breakfast.

"Can this place get any wilder?" Dottye said under her breath, smirking.

As promised, Elsa took us behind the hotel to a beautiful garden where adult tigers and cheetahs were on display in cages. Elsa talked to each cat as if they were her babies. "Aren't they beautiful?" she remarked. They were truly magnificent, but I couldn't help feeling sorry for these beautiful creatures locked behind bars.

Elsa then insisted on giving us a full tour of the hotel

before our limo was scheduled to arrive. She took pride in showing us each of the themed rooms on the lower floor of the hotel.

"This is our 50s room." She beamed as she pointed to a pink Cadillac that had been converted into a bed. "And this room we call the Valentine Room," she continued as she motioned to the heart-shaped bed covered in a red velvet duvet with fur pillows. One room had nothing but steel tables and contraptions hanging from the ceilings. I didn't have the heart to ask her what the theme was in that room... maybe I didn't want to know.

The limo was waiting for us outside on the drive. We said our goodbyes to Elsa and offered to pay for the room and meals but she wouldn't have it (which was a good thing because we didn't have any money). She gave us both a hearty German hug and then escorted us to the big, white limo. As we were leaving the driveway, two large buses arrived filled with Asian men dressed in black suits, obviously there to do business. It didn't seem odd that none of them had any luggage, for none was required for this visit.

We arrived back at the travel agency and found Wolfgang waiting for us. He asked if we enjoyed our stay, and we didn't have the nerve to tell him about our experience. The truth was, we were both extremely grateful for his generosity. He had been a lifesaver to two young, vulnerable American girls far from home. True to his word, Wolfgang arranged for us to fly back to Los Angeles that very day. We thanked him for his hospitality and asked what we could do in return.

"If you find a totem pole, please send it to me," he replied. "I would love to add it to the wild west room at the hotel."

Unfortunately, we never did find that totem pole.

After our trip to Europe, Dottye and I moved into an apartment near Melrose Avenue. The location was closer to Hollywood and the studios. Dottye continued working as the wardrobe director for three sitcoms, and in addition to dancing, I became the backup singer for a local band called Adonis. One day the lead singer informed us that we were booked to play at the Roxy Theater in West Hollywood.

The Roxy is a famous nightclub on Sunset Strip that opened in the early 70s. Famous names like Neil Young, Genesis, and Peter Gabriel played on the stage along with some of my favorite bands at the time, such as X, Bauhaus, Jane's Addiction, and The Cult. I was so excited that I decided to invite my parents to see the show. They didn't approve of my lifestyle in Los Angeles, so I rarely invited them to any of my shows. I was surprised when they said yes.

Thick smoke filled the air of the club as I looked out over the sea of gothic youth in search of my parents. Girls were adorned in shades of pink and purple hair while many of the guys looked like warriors with their spiked Mohawks, piercings, and tattoos. Black was the traditional club attire, so keeping with the trend, I wore a black leather miniskirt, black bustier, fishnets, and my favorite black-and-white stilettos with a steel toe, which I adoringly referred to as my "cockroach killers."

Backstage, I waited nervously for the show to begin. I wondered if Mom and Dad were sitting in the crowd and what they were thinking. I knew this venue was out of their comfort zone—as a matter of fact, way out! My nervous stomach was filled with butterflies, but once the music started, I felt a surge of adrenaline and the butterflies disappeared. Singing at the Roxy was pure magic, almost like an out-of-body experience. The combination of the lights, music, and crowd was intoxicating.

When the show was over, I anxiously looked for Mom and Dad, excited to get their opinion. I felt like a ten-year-old child after a dance recital who needed her Mommy and Daddy's approval. The first words out of Mom's mouth were, "This place is evil, I need to get out of here." Her words cut me to my core, and I could feel myself holding back tears. It was not the reaction I was looking for, but it didn't surprise me. Mom saw the darkness that I could no longer see because I was living it.

It has been said that no light is ever seen without first knowing the darkness, and I was beginning to lose my light and lose my way. Performing at night in the club scene introduced me to a whole new world. I spent less time auditioning for dance gigs and more time partying. An old German proverb says, "When a dove begins to associate with crows, its feathers remain white, but its heart grows black." My conscience was taking a back seat to my ego and "eat, drink, and be merry" was becoming my motto as I crept into a world of sex, drugs, and rock 'n' roll.

The mistakes I made were all part of the lessons I needed to learn to grow. My experiences in the City of Angels eventually led to feelings of unhappiness, confusion, and isolation. There was nowhere to go but up from here.

Chapter 5
Angels and Satan

ALGONAN

"You are always protected. I have shielded you
throughout your life from darkness.
You are a Lightworker."

"In the beginning, God created a world of duality.
Out of darkness came light. It is within the law of
duality that one finds balance and equilibrium. In a
world of dualities, one must place great emphasis
on living in harmony with heaven and earth. When
you see all as one, duality disappears."
—The White Angels

In his book *God's Message to the World*, Neale Donald Walsch provides the following acronym for SATAN: Seeing Any Thing As Negative. Satan, we are lead to believe, is the cause of all evil. He is known by many names—Prince of Darkness, Satan, the devil, Lucifer, the fallen angel. He is described as the enemy of God and, therefore, the enemy of mankind. Whether Satan exists is up for debate, but I question if we have made Satan a "fall guy" for which we can blame our actions and not take responsibility for the horrific atrocities committed by man.

In March 2009, in Washington State, a sixty-two-year-old woman was charged with stealing over $73,000 from her church. During the interrogation, she said, "Satan had a big part in the theft." She passed the blame to something else, which allowed her to become a victim—albeit a victim of Satan, but a victim nonetheless. In the 1970s, comedian and actor Flip Wilson coined the phrase "The devil made me do it," and it was always a hit with the audience. My brothers and I used the phrase to get us out of trouble, and as you can imagine it never worked with our parents.

I was in sixth grade when I had my first experience with darkness. The book *The Exorcist* was creating a lot of attention, and all of my friends were talking about it. My best friend, Chris, let me borrow her book, and I knew I would be in serious trouble if Mom and Dad discovered it. Each night after kneeling in family prayer, I climbed in bed, crawled under the covers with a flashlight, and secretly read about the devil. I was taught that the devil or Satan was a fallen angel. His sole purpose was to keep us mortals from reaching heaven and returning to God. Reading about him made me feel very nervous and uneasy. The deeper I immersed myself in the book, the more frightened I became. Feeling a bit of peer pressure to finish the book, I continued night after night with ever-increasing apprehension and fear.

One night after kneeling in family prayer, I kissed Mom and Dad good night and sauntered off to bed. I turned out the lights, all except for the little night-light that illuminated the corner of the room. Disappearing under the covers, I opened the forbidden book. I began reading about an exorcism the priest was performing on a young girl, and I could picture it implicitly in my mind. The girl in the book was close to my age, which made it even more real. I continued to read while my heart pounded loudly in my chest, and I suddenly felt overcome by darkness. Paralyzed by fear, I sat frozen in terror. I wanted desperately to scream but I was unable to open my mouth. Minutes seemed like hours as I was completely swallowed up by the abyss of evil.

I heard it said in church that if you are confronted by the devil you should say, "In the name of Jesus Christ, I command you to get behind me, Satan." I commanded the darkness to leave, in the name of Jesus Christ, and immediately felt better. I threw off the blankets and made a mad dash for my little brother Scottie's room. Seven years my junior, I held Scottie tight that night and for the next few years slept with him every night, too scared to sleep alone. I threw the book away and, fortunately, Mom and Dad never found out (until now!).

Years later when I was living in Los Angeles, I willingly allowed darkness into my life. Little by little, I found myself falling into the quagmire of vice. It crept in like a "wolf in sheep's clothing," and once immersed, I was forced to swim upstream against the current of life and suffered because of it. I had no one to blame but myself. It would take a few years before I was ready to see the light of change. Darkness is merely the lack of light. Darkness is dispelled at once by bringing in the light, not by chasing the darkness out. When you walk into a dark room and turn on the light, the darkness disappears completely.

Thoughts of fear, hate, and anger bring more darkness and negativity into our lives and the result is suffering. There are many sources of negativity that bombard us daily through the media, television, movies, books, and the Internet. It is important not to get caught up in the frenzy and drama of it all. I decided many years ago to stop watching the news because it created so much fear and sadness in me. I found that by watching violence on TV and in movies, the images became imprinted in my mind forever and thus created a living hell for me. I am now very careful to choose books, music, and movies that have a positive message and high vibration. The White Angels shine light on this very subject.

> "The darkest moment came when humankind chose to use atomic energy to destroy others. As a result, there was a universal call to God to send more light to the planet. Since that time, there has been a shift to light. This light will continue to grow, eliminating darkness and ignorance. All things must choose to move to the light or be lost. Nothing can remain centered around darkness including institutions, governments, individuals, and religions. They must all move to the light or be lost. Mother Nature will choose to purify herself through natural disasters.
> Humankind can begin moving to the light by replacing negative thoughts with positive thoughts; there is nothing to fear. It begins with the one. One individual can influence many, and many individuals

can influence institutions, media, governments, and religions."
— The White Angels

I have learned that I am more help to the world when I feel at peace by keeping my mind focused on the positive and beautiful things that life offers. It is true that we create our own heaven or hell here on earth by the choices we make. Could it be that once we live in harmony with heaven and earth, Satan disappears? Billy Graham, the Christian evangelist, was quoted in *Time* magazine (November 15, 1993) as saying: "The only thing I could say for sure is that hell means separation from God. We are separated from his light, from his fellowship. That is going to be hell... When it comes to a literal fire, I don't preach it because I'm not sure about it."

The White Angels do not refer to hell as we know it, but they do equate hell with suffering. In the Buddhist tradition, one is encouraged to explore what suffering is and the root causes of suffering. The Hindu religion refers to suffering as *Maya*, or cosmic illusion. They believe this veil of Maya obscures our vision of God and creates a living hell for us until we can free ourselves from bondage through right thinking and actions.

It is not God's will that you should suffer. Suffering comes from living in fear and allowing lower vibrating emotions to control the mind. Emotions such as hate, anger, jealousy, resentment, denial, unworthiness, discouragement, and worry—these are seeds of destruction to the mind. Once nourished through wrong thoughts and actions, they grow into disease, unhappiness, and suffering. If these seeds of destruction are not plucked from the mind and cauterized by love, a life of suffering ensues. These seeds can continue lifetime after lifetime if not addressed.

> "Release the grip of negativity and unhappiness that binds you. Do not complain, children, or mutter against one another. Be ever cautious to avoid the vibration the victim mentality brings, for it is a trap of delusion that will keep one on the wheel of suffering. Apply the balm of understanding to your differences. See each other through the eyes of God. Suffer no more. Ask God and the angels to help you learn the lessons in your suffering necessary for you to excel forward in your life."
> — The White Angels

Delusion and ignorance are a facade that mask the light of hope and knowledge. Ignorance causes us to fear the unknown, that which we do not understand. "Ignorance is not bliss," as the old saying goes. It is only through awareness and knowledge that we begin to understand there is nothing to fear because we live in a benevolent universe. In 1967, George Harrison wrote in his song "Within You Without You" the following lines: "And the people that hid themselves behind a wall of illusion / Never glimpse the truth / Then it's far too late when they pass away."

The White Angels tell me that fear is the opposite of love. This surprised me, because I thought hate was the opposite of love. But according to the angels, fear carries the lowest vibration of all emotions.

> "Only good comes from God. All that is not good originates from delusion and ignorance. What you focus on, you create. Poverty, illness, and war are earth-bound energies that carry very low vibrating frequencies. They are not from God but are fear-

based thoughts and actions. Fear is the opposite of love. It is the lack of love. Fear is darkness, and darkness is delusion."
— The White Angels

In my experience, I have found that negative energy can manifest in the form of physical disease to the body. The White Angels say, **"Wrong thoughts and actions grow into disease, unhappiness, and suffering."** It is for this reason that I place a barrier of protection around me in the form of a pyramid of white light when I do Reiki on my clients. This prevents any energy that is not my own from entering my energy field, or aura as it is known. I use this same technique when I know I will be traveling. I also call upon Archangel Michael for protection when I am traveling or anytime I feel vulnerable.

Everyone can call upon Archangel Michael to help watch over and protect you and your loved ones, communities, countries, and the planet. God has given him the responsibility to rid the earth of darkness and fear, so no task is too big for this powerful archangel! It is no wonder he is the patron saint of police officers! I asked Archangel Michael to watch over us on a recent trip my daughters and I took to Europe. He came to our rescue one day on a train in Paris.

The train arrived at the underground station, but the girls and I hesitated to get on. We were not quite sure if it was going to our destination. At the last minute, we decided to go for it and made a mad dash for the doors.

Suddenly, I heard my daughter Tess scream, "Mom, the door closed on my foot!" I was flooded with horror as I turned to see her foot hanging out of the carriage. Pumped full of adrenaline, I struggled to get the doors open. The train began to take off and my heart sunk into my stomach. I immediately began praying and a handsome blond man stood up, calmly opened the doors, and released her foot. He then quietly sat down and nodded, and I thanked him with tears in my eyes.

"It's okay, Mom. I am fine," Tess whispered, aware that all eyes were now on us.

My eyes now flooded with tears. I felt nauseous thinking about what could have happened. The train arrived at our stop, and I thanked the blond man again for his help. I am not sure he understood English, but he certainly could read my emotions. After I said goodbye to him, I heard a whisper in my ear, "I am here to protect you." It was then that I realized the blonde man was Archangel Michael. Before I could turn around to take one last look, the train had left the station. Later that day, I took a picture of the girls standing in front of the statue of Archangel Michael at the Fountain Saint Michel. Now every time I see that picture, I am reminded of that experience and his promise to protect us.

Archangel Michael releases us from negative energy and empowers us with confidence and courage. The following is a meditation I use with my clients to help release any fears holding them back from achieving happiness. The purpose of this meditation is to raise your vibration to the frequency of love, the most powerful force in the universe. Archangel Michael is the most powerful of all archangels. He is the overseer of all Lightworkers (individuals who raise the vibration of the planet by bring light to others through service, peace, and love) and their life's purpose.

Sit in a quiet, comfortable spot. Close your eyes and take in a deep, cleansing breath. As you inhale, visualize filling your body with light and as you exhale release all stress, negativity, and fear. Repeat this breathing exercise three times.

1. Call on Archangel Michael: "Archangel Michael, please come to me now." Take a moment to feel his presence (you might feel heat or warmth).

2. Know that Archangel Michael is now beside you. He is here to help release any fears that you are holding onto, fears that keep you from living a complete and happy life. Ask Archangel Michael to help release any fears of lack, unworthiness, money, abundance, expectation of others, emotional entanglements, and all other fears that you are consciously or unconsciously aware of. Take a deep breath... inhale, exhale.

3. Repeat these words: "Archangel Michael, please release me from any negative energy I have taken from places, situations, relationships, and things. Archangel Michael, please free me from fear of sharing my God-given gifts to the world, and fill me with courage and confidence to share my talents with others." Take a deep breath... inhale, exhale.

4. Continue: "Archangel Michael, please fill me with love, prosperity, confidence, and joy. Surround me in a pyramid of powerful, white light that will protect me and keep me safe. Thank you." And so it is.

5. Now take in a deep, cleansing breath. Thank Archangel Michael for his divine help in raising your vibration. Inhale this new vibration of love and light and release anything that does not serve your greatest and highest good, releasing all tension and worldly cares. Take another deep breath.

You may do this meditation as often as you need to help release any negativity and raise your vibration.

The decision to live a life filled with love and light or negativity and darkness rests fully upon each of us. God gave us free will to make our own choices, and we will live according to those choices. It is up to us to find balance and equilibrium in the dual nature of this universe. When we live in harmony with heaven and earth, that balance is maintained. If we choose not to, then we suffer.

> "Know that all is not as it seems. Reality is a delusion veiled by the ignorance of man, blanketed by fear. Once unconditional love becomes the primary frequency on earth, darkness and ignorance will be lifted, and the mysteries of the universe made known. Until that time, trust your intuition. Listen to no man but answer only to God."
> — The White Angels

Chapter 6
Angels and Synchronicities

SARAHI

"Do not live in the past, it prevents you from moving forward. Open your understanding... there is so much more."

"We must be willing to get rid of the life we've planned, so as to have the life that is waiting for us."
—Joseph Campbell

Carl Jung called synchronicities "meaningful coincidences." Merriam-Webster's dictionary defines synchronicities as "the coincidental occurrence of events and especially psychic events (as similar thoughts in widely separated persons or a mental image of an unexpected event before it happens) that seem related but are not explained by conventional mechanisms of causality." In his book *Messages from Water and the Universe*, Dr. Masaru Emoto calls synchronicities "God's kind arrangement."

Angels arrange opportunities and events for us as answers to prayers. These synchronicities move us forward on our life path. Sometimes we think we know what is best for our lives when in actuality it takes us away from our life purpose. You might have a plan, but if you give it over to God and listen to the guidance of your angels, you will find your plan pales in comparison to God's.

When we open ourselves up to universal energy, the more synchronicities will flow into our lives. Wayne Dyer explained this when he said the following: "The universe is complete and perfect. There can be no mistakes. Nothing is random. The entire 'onesong' is exquisitely synchronized. To understand synchronicity and to implement it, we are required to suspend some of our old ideas, to give up our notion of coincidence of mistakes, our belief that people are imperfect."

> "When you ask the angels to bring more abundance
> to your life, you set in motion a series of events
> that you might refer to as synchronicities. We
> work through people, places, and things to bring
> opportunities to you that will result in abundance."
> — The White Angels

Angels work on our behalf through people, places, and things. They are ever near, always trying to get our attention. Butterflies, hummingbirds, and feathers are a few ways the angels let us know they are near. Early one morning at 3:00 a.m., I was awakened by the White Angels and instructed to go into my meditation room. It was a bit chilly, so I grabbed a sweater coat in the closet and wrapped it around me. I lit candles and incense to prepare for meditation and sat down on the floor with my legs crossed. Before I closed my eyes, I looked down and noticed a beautiful, vibrant blue feather sitting in my lap. It came out of nowhere, a lovely reminder that my angels were in the room with me.

Waking up at three in the morning is not a coincidence, but a synchronicity. I began waking up every morning between three and four when I first started communicating with angels. They explained to me that this is a time when the veil between heaven and earth is thinnest. Dr. Wayne Dyer referred to the hours between 3:00 and 4:00 a.m. as a time "when we are close to Source, and a great time of inspiration and creativity." The yogis in India call this time of day *Brahmamuhurta*, or the Creator's hour. These are the last three hours of the night between 3:00 a.m. and 6:00 a.m. In yoga, these auspicious hours are considered the most suitable for meditation and prayer. The ancient Sufi mystic Rumi spoke of these early morning hours: "The breeze at dawn has secrets to tell you. Don't go back to sleep. You must ask for what you really want. Don't go back to sleep. People are going back and forth across the doorsill where the two worlds touch. The door is round and open. Don't go back to sleep."

Our guardian angels are constantly trying to communicate with us. Whether it is a feather in your lap or a song on the radio, it is up to us to pay attention. I often ask the angels to send me a message through lyrics in songs. I did this one day while I was driving down the freeway. When I turned on the radio, the song was so beautiful I started to cry. Since that day, I began creating an "angel playlist" so that I can hear the messages again and again. Thomas Carlyle said, "Music is well said to be the speech of angels." Throughout history, artists have depicted angels holding a variety of instruments from the harp to the trumpet. I have a statue of an angel playing the lute hanging on my wall. She is a replica of the original woodcarving found at Saint Giles' Cathedral in Edinburgh, Scotland, and a beautiful reminder for me to listen to my angels.

Numbers and number sequences are another way angels communicate with us. A sequence of numbers is not just a coincidence. For example, the number four is referred to as the angelic number. Have you ever looked at a clock at exactly 4:44? (As I write this, the time is 4:04 p.m.) Each number vibrates at a certain frequency and therefore carries a certain meaning. This is the science of numerology, the study of numbers and their divine significance. It is based on the theory that the universe is mathematically precise, and each number holds a certain vibration. Pythagoras, the Greek mathematician, believed that numbers have positive and negative qualities. He also believed that each number has a divine origin with coinciding events associated with it. So the next time you see a sequence of numbers, know that the angels are nearby with a special message.

Music and numbers are a few of the signs angels use to communicate with us. Angels use signs to communicate because of the vibrational variance between us. Our physical bodies do not vibrate at the same frequency as angels or other divine beings, so we may not see or hear them, but we can keep our eyes and ears open to their divine signs. (Frequency is the rate at which a vibration occurs that constitutes a wave, either in a material or in an electromagnetic field.)

Awareness is the first step in following our heavenly guidance and then acknowledging that guidance as divine intervention is the second step. Thanking God and the angels for the help you receive is the final and, I believe, most important step. When we give thanks with a full heart we open up the opportunities to receive more blessings and abundance from the universe.

"Signs from above come in numerous ways. Heaven communicates to each one in the way they are best able to receive the message. This varies with each individual depending on their vibration and openness to receive. Angels communicate through sequences of numbers, feathers, and messages in books and other publications. Messages can be received through lyrics in songs or from other individuals sent from the angels. Events that seem coincidental are arranged on your behalf by the angels. Serendipitous events line up so you can meet a soulmate, change your career, or find the perfect home.

"Some are able to feel the presence of an angel by a ringing in the ears or a warm embrace when there is no one around. Those with heightened awareness may have the ability to hear angels, see angels, and feel the angels near. All have these abilities, yet it takes time and effort to raise the vibration to receive these signs and communications from above. The ability to receive lies in the frequency at which one vibrates. The higher the vibration, the greater the ability to receive communication.

"The key to receiving signs from above is in awareness. Be aware of your surroundings. There are no coincidences in life. Angels are often orchestrating on your behalf behind the scenes, so do not be afraid to ask. Always thank God and the angels for showing you signs and answering your prayers. Gratitude opens the windows of heaven."

— The White Angels

My life has been full of synchronicities and coincidences, opportunities and chance meetings. Two of the biggest events in my life were completely orchestrated by the angelic realm and a great example of how synchronicity works. In both cases, by "letting go and letting God," my life turned out better than I could have ever imagined.

The first event turned my life upside down. It was September 11, 2001, and I was watching the morning news. Suddenly there was a news flash and images of the Twin Towers in New York up in flames appeared onscreen. The US president delivered a statement that the World Trade Center had been hit in an apparent terrorist attack. I remember sitting in front of the TV in complete disbelief that anything like this could happen on US soil. The images on TV were surreal, almost as if I was watching a war movie. A resounding "Why?" kept repeating in my head. 9/11 had a tremendous effect on our country. We would never be the same again. It also had a direct impact on my life.

Around the time of 9/11, I was working for the Jewish Federation of Greater Los Angeles as the health and fitness director in one of their main centers. After the incident, the Federation announced that they were closing many of the centers. Our center was on the list, and I was devastated by the news. How would I support my children as a single mother without a job? It felt like the world was crashing down around me. After eighteen years, I decided it was to leave my beloved City of Angels. It was time to go home to San Diego, but I needed to find a job and sell my home in LA to make the move. I didn't know that as my world was caving in on me, my angels were working diligently behind the scene on my behalf.

Opportunities lined up for me that could only have been orchestrated in heaven. Within one month, I sold my home in Los Angeles and started a new job in San Diego. I was offered a position in Rancho Santa Fe as the Spa and Fitness Director at the Bridges, a very exclusive golfing community north of San Diego. The Bridges Clubhouse looked like a grand Italian castle nestled somewhere in the hills of Tuscany. Vineyards provided a backdrop to a stunning golf course where two suspended bridges floated in the air as if by magic. The stately clubhouse drive was lined with Bentleys and Ferraris that sparkled like jewels. Far removed from the traffic and chaos of Los Angeles, this paradise was truly the work of angels.

The second example of how synchronicity has impacted my life happened in Sin City... Las Vegas, Nevada. I was attending a spa convention with my friend, an esthetician who worked for me at the Bridges Spa. It happened to be her birthday, and she was excited to mix business with pleasure. After a long day at the convention, we decided to have dinner at Planet Hollywood Resort and Casino, where we were staying, to celebrate her birthday.

Stepping into the elevators at Planet Hollywood is a sensory explosion. Mirrors line the walls and ceiling, and music blasts from the speakers. Elton John was playing when we stepped into the empty elevator, and the song took me back to my high school days. I was lost in a 70s flashback when the elevator door suddenly opened and a very distinguished gentleman entered.

"Good evening," he said. "Are you ladies going somewhere?"

"Yes, we are going to dinner to celebrate her birthday," I said as I felt my face flush.

"Then you should probably push the button," he said with a slight grin on his face.

In our excitement, we failed to push the button and had gone nowhere fast. After a good laugh, he proceeded to push the button for us, and I got a good look at him. He was tall, had black hair, and was wearing a grey suit, white shirt, and tie. I felt my face flush and my body tingle with goose bumps.

The elevator stopped and before he stepped out, he turned to us. "Ladies, have a wonderful evening, and happy birthday," he said, nodding at my friend. Then he handed me his Planet Hollywood business card and encouraged us to call him if we needed anything during our stay. He was gone as quickly as he appeared.

She wasn't sure what was happening, but she could sense a shift had taken place in me.

"What's wrong with you?" she yelled over the loud music.

"I'm not sure," I replied. What I didn't tell her was that I knew one day I was going to marry that man. Four years later, Joe and I had a fairytale wedding in the Bahamas.

Meeting Joe in the elevator that day was truly "God's kind arrangement." I never expected to find my soulmate in Las Vegas, and quite honestly it would have been the last place I would have looked. They say that "timing is everything," and the day I met Joe was divine timing.

I am sure if you think back to the pivotal moments in your life, you too will see the hand of God and angels at work. Joe and I joke to this day that my Great Aunt Norma and his mother, June, were the two behind our meeting. I am sure they were smiling down upon us the day we were married along with a host of angels. Our wedding pictures are filled with orbs, proof that our spirit guides and angels were with us. The next time you have a remarkable coincidence of events or circumstances, don't forget to thank your angels. As Deepak Chopra says, "Coincidences are not accidents but signals from the universe which can guide us toward our true destiny."

Chapter 7

Angels and Spirit Guides

TIMOTHY

"Listen with your heart, for it is there you
will find your answers."

**"People are unaware that spirits even exist, let alone
that angels are present with them."
—Emanuel Swedenborg**

I am often asked what the difference is between angels
and spirit guides. Spirit guides have had a physical body
and angels (for the most part) do not. Because of this, they

vibrate at different frequencies. We have countless angels and spirit guides working with us to guide our path. Unlike guardian angels, we do not choose our spirit guides and they do not stay with us for the duration of our lifetime. It is part of their training to learn how to guide and inspire us. Spirit guides come and go as we need them, assisting us with specific projects or events.

Our spirit guides can be a dear aunt or perhaps someone we have never met before. Benjamin Franklin guided my oldest daughter Haley during her first year in law school. I saw him while I was giving her Reiki one day. He appeared along with four other men all dressed in dark suits (the suits looked like they could have been in fashion a few hundred years ago). Mr. Franklin explained to me that he and these other men would be helping Haley with her law studies. I assumed that the other men had some experience in law during a past life, though I could not identify them. As a mother, it gave me great comfort knowing she was in good hands.

I met two of my spirit guides when I became a Reiki practitioner. The day I became a Reiki master, Mother Teresa appeared to me during a meditation. Her countenance was bright and powerful though her size was frail and petite. She explained that I had been called to serve others, and she would be guiding my healing work. I asked her how she was able to work with the sick and dying and she replied, "I protect myself in Jesus." She explained that she dedicated all her work in his name. She also advised me to close my Manipura chakra (third chakra located at the solar plexus) when I work with the sick. "It is where energy exchange takes place," she said lovingly.

Sai is another spirit guide who revealed herself to me. Sai lived in Japan during WWII and told me she was killed during the attack on Hiroshima. She explained that at that time, Reiki was practiced primarily in Japan and was not known to the rest of the world as it is today. She related that many Reiki masters, like her, were killed because of the war. (The White Angels have told me that the dropping of the atomic bomb was the darkest moment in this planet's history.) Sai was sent to help guide my Reiki healings and oversee my practice. Her energy is very soft and gentle.

"When someone dies, an angel is there to meet them at the gates of Heaven to let them know that their life has just begun." —Anonymous

We often feel our loved ones near us once they cross over. This does not necessarily mean they are here to guide as our spirit guide; they just want to be near us, or perhaps they have a message for us. This was the case with my beloved Great Aunt Norma, who was like a mother to me. Aunt Norma battled cancer and won four times. Her determined nature and stubbornness prevented the disease from getting the best of her. It was only when she was diagnosed with a brain tumor in 2005 that she finally gave in. She was tired of fighting. I had the privilege of being with her at the end of her life.

I spent days by her side with the care of a kind hospice nurse.

"You have to tell her it is okay to leave," the nurse said. "She is holding on for you and her husband."

Selfishly, I didn't want her to go, and I knew Uncle

Jimmy didn't either. I had never been this close to death before, and I wasn't sure how to handle it. "Hold my hand," Aunt Norma said. I held her hand gently, but it felt cool. She dozed in and out, her breathing faint. Lying in her bed, she whispered, "I have been to the place I am supposed to go."

"Where did you go, Aunt Norma?" I asked, but she continued to repeat the same sentence again. I questioned her about the place, and if she saw anything there.

She looked at me with glazed-over eyes and replied, "I am confused."

With tears in my eyes, I said softly, "It is okay to stay in that place. You don't need to come back." I told her how much I loved her and kissed her on the cheek. She dozed off again and when she woke, she was speaking to her father, calling him by name. I knew that he was in the room with us and that he had come to take her home. I could feel the energy in the room shift, and I knew the angels were nearby. She took her last breath gracefully, and with a look of peace and serenity she left her body.

As I write this book, Uncle Jimmy, Aunt Norma's husband, recently passed on. He waited ten years before he was ready to join her. I was fortunate to be by his bedside the day he died, too. I put a golden egg around him and filled it with Reiki energy to assist him with the process of crossing over. I could see Aunt Norma and his brother Jack in the room waiting for him from the other side. I knew the time was very close. That evening he left his body and was once again reunited with his friends and family. A few weeks after he passed, he came to me and thanked me, expressing his love and gratitude.

It is important when our loved ones die that we do not hold onto our grief, for this can sometimes keep them from crossing to the light. Ask the angels to help you lovingly release them so that you can heal the wounds of separation. We are never truly separate, as we are all eternal beings, and you will one day be reunited with them. This is also true for our pets. The White Angels have shared the following message about animals: **"Many times a pet will remain close to his human companion after passing. They anxiously wait to once again reunite with their beloved on the other side. Sometimes they choose not to wait and will reappear in your current life again in a different body."**

Spirits that do not go immediately to the light are referred to as earthbound spirits. Earthbound spirits fail to cross over for various reasons; perhaps their death was unexpected or traumatic, or they feel guilty or remorseful for something they have done while living. Many spirits are unable to release earthly attachments that keep them from moving forward. These attachments could be anything from addiction, family and friends, material wealth, to possessions. My good friend Karl is instrumental in helping earthbound spirits cross over. Because of a near-death experience he had as a toddler, Karl has seen spirits from a very early age. Many earthbound spirits have come to him that felt lost or confused and unable to go into the light. I experienced his abilities one evening during dinner.

I was dining with Karl and my friend Sonia at our favorite restaurant on the beach. Enjoying another breathtaking orange and purple sunset, we watched as the sun slowly lowered beyond the horizon. It was Christmas time, and the restaurant sparkled with silver and gold decorations, and Christmas music played in the background. My daughter Haley had recently suffered the loss of a dear friend due to a drug overdose, and she was devastated by his death. I was recounting the tragic story of this young boy when suddenly my face became flushed and my breathing difficult. It felt like someone was standing on my chest. My throat began to tighten and my head was pounding.

"What's wrong?" Sonia could tell I was struggling.

"I'm not sure. It's probably just a hot flash," I joked.

"You have a young man standing next to you," Karl said. He described him, and it matched the description of the boy that had just passed away. "He is angry about his death and is telling me it was all a big mistake. His death was an accident." Karl explained that the boy was unable to cross over due to the sorrow and guilt he felt for the pain he caused his family. This guilt was keeping him from the light. He clarified that his death was not suicide but the wrong combination of drugs and alcohol taken while partying. Karl explained that by discussing the young man I had called him in and now he was using me to communicate with Karl. Karl told the young man he could help him and asked him to follow him home later after dinner.

Immediately I began to feel physical relief; however, I was a bit shaken by the experience. I felt deep empathy for the parents of this young boy. As a mother, I could not imagine the grief and pain they were experiencing. Karl called me later that evening with good news that he successfully assisted the young man in crossing over. "An older man came to escort him to the light, most likely a relative of his, maybe an uncle or grandfather," he exclaimed gleefully. I was happy to hear the news and shared it with my daughter, who cried tears of joy. It reaffirmed to her that he had not attempted suicide, and that knowledge helped to heal her wounds. Later that week, he came to her in a dream. In the dream, he assured her that he was okay and asked her not to worry or be sad for him anymore.

When we leave this earth, we can return again depending on our karma. Paramahansa Yogananda explained karma in this way: "Karma is the law of action or cosmic justice, based upon cause and effect. Your every act, good or bad, has a specific effect on your life... Karma decrees that as one sows, so must he inevitably reap... Persons who pass their lifetime satisfying the body and gratifying the ego, unaware of the divine image in themselves, amass earthly karma, or sins. When they die with those unresolved karmic consequences and with unfulfilled earthly desires, they must reincarnate again and again to resolve all mortal entanglements."

"The law of cause and effect is how one pays universal debts to another. If you have caused harm to any living creature, you must make amends in this lifetime or the next. One chooses where birth will take place and who the parents will be. Some choose to be born disabled for greater growth and learning for oneself and loved ones. You bring into your current life the emotional energy at the time of passing from the previous life. For example, if you were fearful at the time of your death, you will bring that fear energy into your next incarnation. This energy is stored in your subtle or astral body. This is also true of any physical injuries you sustained in a past life that were not healed at the time of death. This area will be a point of weakness in the physical body in your present incarnation. This is why many are born with addictions and others are not. Addictions are the emotions caused from lack of self-love in a previous life or self-punishment. It is true that the lessons you do not learn in this life will be taught again in the next. It is the result of a just and benevolent universe to teach in such a kind and loving way. One has only to grasp this concept to be free from the cycle of repetition."

—The White Angels

Chapter 8
Angels Help

VIVICA & DANIEL

"Have faith and trust. Be true to who you are."

"If angels come not to minister us, it is because we
do not invite them, it is because we keep the door
closed through which they might otherwise enter."
—**Ralph W. Trine**

The "law of free will" prevents angels from interfering
with our lives (with the exception of our guardian angel if

it is not our time to die). Therefore, it is imperative that we ask the angels for help in all things. As I write this book I have called in the angels to help guide and inspire my words.

> "If one thinks about angels or asks for their help, angels immediately respond according to God's will and only for your greatest and highest good."
> —The White Angels

"For your greatest and highest good" are the key words here, because although angels are available to help us, it might not be for your greatest and highest good to win the lottery. Sorry!

We can call upon the angels for help with everything, from our most important questions to ordinary and mundane tasks. I am finally in the habit of asking for help from the parking angels when looking for a place to park. It has saved me time and frustration knowing that when I get to my destination I will have a parking spot waiting for me. During the holidays, I ask for angelic guidance in finding the perfect gift for those on my list. It works every time! Your life will change significantly when you begin calling upon the angels for help. There are many unemployed angels out there merely because we do not ask for their assistance. Never worry that they are too busy—multitudes of angels are standing by, waiting to help.

My daughter Tess and I called upon the angels to help us when she was involved in a car accident a few years ago. Tess was driving home from church on a Sunday afternoon when another car hit hers. My husband and I were not far behind her, but we did not actually see the accident.

It wasn't until we came upon her totaled vehicle that we realized it was Tess. Standing in the middle of the road, she looked completely bewildered and disoriented. Joe pulled over and I jumped out of our car and rushed to her side, my motherly instincts kicking into emergency mode. Holding her in my arms, she began to cry. Unhurt but in shock, I put her safely inside our car and proceeded to speak to the woman who had hit her.

Fortunately, there was a witness to the accident. The gentleman approached me, introduced himself as John, and then handed me his card. "I saw the woman hit your daughter's car. I am so sorry. I hope she is not hurt," he said. I looked at the card and saw his last name was Trafficanada. Was this a joke? *Anada* in Hindi means "bliss." Was his name really "trafficbliss?" I thanked Mr. Trafficanada and told him we would call him if we needed any further assistance. When I turned around, there was no sign of him anywhere, which leads me to believe he was an angel sent to assist.

Thanks to God and the angels, Tess was unharmed in the accident, but her car was beyond repair. The time came to shop for a new car, so Tess and I visited a dealership nearby. I dreaded the process of buying a car, so I asked the angels to help us find the right car for Tess.

We drove to a local dealership and a car salesman came up to greet us. "Hi, my name is Angel. How can I help you today?" he said, smiling.

Tess and I laughed at each other and said, "Of course it is!" Angel was true to his name and moved heaven and earth to get my daughter an amazing deal. All we had to do was ask!

Many of my clients come seeking guidance from the angels. One of the biggest questions I hear repeatedly is "How can I create more abundance in my life?" These clients feel stuck in the financial cycle of debt and unable to free themselves. They are not aware they are blocking abundance from coming into their lives by their own thoughts and opinions about it.

Unfortunately, many people equate abundance to money and sabotage their prosperity by activating the lack mentally (feeling as though there is not enough to go around). It is true that money holds a specific vibration. We either put ourselves in a vibrational match to receive it or repel it. When we align ourselves with the belief that the universe provides us with everything we need, including money, we become a vibrational match to that energy and create more of it in our lives. When we believe that we do not have enough money, we also become a vibrational match to that energy and we experience the lack of it.

"Money is not good or bad; it is just energy. Money is not real or tangible; it is merely a concept with an energy force around it. You attract the force by thinking positive thoughts or you repel it by thinking negative thoughts. Worrying about money activates this energy force negatively and thus creates a lack of money. Keeping your thoughts and vibrations high when thinking of money is important. Doing what you love with the intention to create money will activate the flow of money. However, do not let ego and greed get in the way. Listen to your heart and do only what you love. Always do good things with money, and do not use it to harm others. Change the way you think about money and you will change the energy around it and how it flows to you. Those on earth confuse abundance to be money and material wealth. It is so much more."

— The White Angels

The angels of abundance rejoice in helping us live a more abundant life. They have access to people, places, and things that we do not. Once we allow abundance to flow into our lives, we experience health, prosperity, wisdom, and happiness. Our relationships change for the better and we have more time to do the things we love. The White Angels tell us the meaning of abundance is "**All good things come from God.**" When we truly believe this and align ourselves to this vibration, the portals of heaven will open and God's blessings will flow abundantly.

"Abundance means all things good come from God. This includes love, harvest, friendship, blessings, health, beauty, families, knowledge, truth, peace, and freedom. To live an abundant life is to live a balanced life rich with these universal gifts. To be wealthy without peace, truth, or friendship is not living in abundance. The law of attraction is like a magnet. If it is truth you seek, you must be truthful. You cannot merely wish abundance into your life. Like all universal laws, it must be activated. The law of abundance is activated through your thoughts. The universe brings you more of what you are thinking. If you are thinking love, it will bring you more love. If you are thinking fearful thoughts, it will bring more fear into your life. The law of attraction does not discriminate.

"God's universe is a loving universe and abundant universe. There are many angels of abundance actively working to bring greater good and happiness to your lives at this time. Do not feel that all good comes through hard work. Let us make it easier for you by asking for our assistance. We can accomplish from our heavenly realm what you cannot from where you are. We rejoice in this work. Pray often the prayer of abundance: 'Angels, please bless me with abundance so I may share it with others, and so it is.'"

— The White Angels

Health is another area where my clients want answers from the angels. Some are struggling to lose weight and cannot seem to find the motivation to exercise, while others have chronic back pain or physical afflictions that prevent them from experiencing life to the fullest. Still, others suffer from depression and anxiety and want to avoid taking medication, so they look to the angels for guidance. Any imbalance in our physical or emotional body caused by negative thoughts will lower our vibrations. All disease is rooted in the mind, and if we let negative emotions fester, they will eventually manifest as physical maladies and disease.

Positive affirmations are a powerful way we can use our words to bring health and wellness to our body and mind. Paramahansa Yogananda once said, "Sincere words or affirmations repeated understandingly, feelingly, and willingly are sure to move the Omnipresent Cosmic Vibratory Force to render aid in your difficulty." Choose an affirmation that applies to your current condition. For example, if you suffer from anxiety you could affirm the following: "I love and approve of myself. I am safe, all is well." Make sure that you wholeheartedly believe the affirmation and have faith it will help your situation, permitting no doubt or disbelief. Repeat the affirmation upon waking each day and before going to bed at night so that it penetrates your conscious and subconscious mind.

If you suffer from physical or mental conditions, ask the angels to help you align with the vibration of perfect health and well-being. If we are not in harmony with our mind and body, our spirit cannot expand to its fullest potential. The angels instruct us to keep our body and mind pure, as it is the vehicle that houses our soul. The White Angels have given explicit instruction on the proper care of our "Body Temple."

> "The body is a gift from God to each spirit child to be used during the time of birth until the time of death. It is a temporary vehicle in which the soul is housed during each incarnation. It is precious and miraculous. It is to be honored and respected, yet not to be adored. The body temple has been misunderstood by mankind. Most believe it to be their identity due to the loss of knowledge of who they really are. Some become attached and obsessed with the body, and others neglect or abuse the body temple.

> "When one is aligned with the vibration of God, one understands the purpose for this Divine creation. To attain this understanding is to be in awe of the magnificence of the body temple and yet not to worship it as many do. God alone is worshipped.

> "Maintaining the body temple is of paramount importance. This means cleansing the body daily with water that is blessed. Thank the water for washing away all impurities from the body and removing all toxins and lower vibrations from the skin. Nourish the body with only high vibrating foods. Drink more water than you think you need.

Bless all food and water before it enters the body temple and give thanks to God for providing for your needs. Treat the body as you would a fine coat, one that covers and protects you. Communicate with the body. Do not indulge the body in overeating, as it will tire the body before it's time.

"The body was designed to move, walk, run, swim, and dance. In order to keep the body vibrating at its optimal frequency, the body must move daily and joyfully. The mind and the body work synergistically, communicating as one. One does not dictate to the other. Be aware of this delicate balance and listen to what your body is saying. Do not discount the subtle messages from the body when it is communicating through physical manifestations. Discord between mind and body will eventually lead to disease. It is for this reason one must be aware of the needs and not the wants of the mind and body and administer to it accordingly.

"Through constant and loving care by daily cleansing, eating high-vibrational foods, drinking an abundance of water, and moving the body, the body temple will vibrate at the highest frequency, allowing the soul to expand, grow, and accomplish wonderful things. Give thanks to God daily for the blessings of the body temple, and honor it as a priceless gift from the Creator."
—The White Angels

Ultimately, we are all seeking happiness. The search for happiness is the greatest common denominator in all of us and is our God-given right. Many seek happiness from the material world, such as a new car or home. Some believe finding the perfect relationship or the next big promotion will make them happy. Happiness seems to linger somewhere out there in the future for many. My clients come to me hopeful that the angels will guide them in the pursuit of a better life. They often tell me, "I will be happy when this event, relationship, job, or (fill in the blank) happens." They are relying on the outside world to give them what they unknowingly already possess. The search for happiness begins within.

It is God's will that all of his children are happy. However, happiness is a choice. It is a decision you alone make. Lasting happiness does not come from a car, home, job, or lover. Happiness comes from within, not without. You can remain eternally happy even when you are surrounded by chaos if you choose. It is a choice we must make every minute of every day. The White Angels have given these ten steps to create more happiness in your life.

Ten Steps to Happiness

1. Wake each day in gratitude, and go to sleep each night giving thanks.

2. Take time to go within by sitting in silent meditation... find peace.

3. Talk to God, even if you don't know how.

4. Do something for someone else without any thought of receiving in return. Giving to others cleanses the spirit and removes your ego's grip.

5. Raise your vibration.

6. Eat healthy food. Food should be used to bring nutrients to

the body, not pleasure to the mind.

7. Move the body by doing something you love.

8. Socialize. Meet like-minded people.

9. Laugh. Don't take life too seriously (it will be over before you know it!).

10. Decide to be happy. It is a conscious choice.

Happiness comes from helping others and getting involved with something bigger than ourselves. We can make a big difference in the lives of others through our prayers. This not only holds true for our loved ones but for our beloved Mother Earth. She gives to us unconditionally, and one way we can give back is by asking the angels to send love and light to the planet. It doesn't have to be formal, just simply, "Angels, please send love and light to our planet Earth. Surround our world and everyone in it with a powerful pyramid of white light."

> "Connect daily to the earth energy by grounding.
> You come to this incarnation through physical birth,
> and give the body back to Gaia upon departure. Her
> energy sustains the physical body through sunlight,
> water, air, and food. It is therefore of the most
> importance to the physical body that you call to
> her daily and draw upon her energy. Plant your feet
> firmly upon her soil and give thanks in return."
> — The White Angels

When we ask the angels to help others, it is a selfless act and we are blessed in turn. Our requests are so powerful, we have no idea the impact they make. That power is magnified when you gather as a group, for there is truly strength in numbers. Socializing with a group of like-minded souls contributes to our happiness, and as a group we can make a difference in the happiness of others. That is why prayer circles are so important and necessary now in our planet's history. Together, we can send a request for peace and harmony on earth and love and peace to all hearts. As individuals, we can make a significant difference, but as a group, we can change the world.

> "Peace is knowing you are safe, you are whole, and you are connected to Source. You do not find peace, for peace is your divine nature. You must look deep inside to bring peace to the surface and maintain the energy in your daily life. Peace is the natural state of all things in the universe. It is necessary to quiet the mind and remove yourself from the chaos around you to mine the brilliant gem of peace. You will feel it wrap your soul with a divine blanket of love as a child feels cradled in its mother's arms. Peacefulness is a state of feeling safe and completely content deep inside, a knowingness that all is well.

> "This peace energy can be shared with those around you. By merely tapping into your own peace, you will radiate that vibration to others. This is how you will help save the planet from conflict and war. Each individual must find their peace and hold the vibration of peace long enough that it may radiate to others. We cannot place enough importance on this fact. Guard your peace vibration like a precious jewel. Do not give it away to propaganda and fear stories that the world will tell you. It will shatter your peace and lower your vibration.

"Surround yourself with nature, beautiful music, inspiring people, and enlightened literature to hold the vibration of peace consciousness. It only takes a few to spread the vibration of peace to the many. To be at peace with yourself is to be one with God. Ask God and the angels to fill you with peace. Ask for the vibration of peace to fill the hearts of your earthly brothers and sisters. Visualize peace spreading like a field of wild flowers across all lands covering all hearts with its fragrant blooms."

— The White Angels

We have a wealth of divine resources at our fingertips. It is up to us to believe and trust that it is ours. If it is abundance you seek, happiness, health, prosperity, peace, or wisdom, ask the angels. They are here to advise and assist us in all things, but we must ask. Ask with a grateful heart and open mind. Open the door, and they will bring you the answers you are searching for.

Chapter 9
Spiritual Awakening

OPHELIA

"Christ is a guiding presence in your life. Call upon him daily. Study crystals and their healing effects."

"When a man learns to rise above the need for breath, he ascends into the celestial realms of angels."
—Paramahansa Yogananda

We all grow and develop spiritually at our own pace. This evolution cannot be forced or rushed while we explore the truths that resonate with our soul. This process is gently guided by our angels, guides, and ascended masters. My spiritual awakening began when I read the book *Autobiography of a Yogi* by Paramahansa Yogananda. They say when the student is ready, the teacher appears.

I was at a pivotal point in my life, divorced with two young daughters to take care of, and I felt lost and insecure. Prayer was something I practiced daily, but learning how to meditate opened up a new world for me. The more I looked within for the answers, the less I relied on external sources. The main obstacle to my spiritual progression was my ego. I love the quote by Marianne Williamson, "Ego says, 'Once everything falls into place, I'll feel peace.' Spirit says, 'Find your peace, and then everything will fall into place.'"

My ego was never at peace! Proud as a peacock and fierce as a lion, nothing but perfection would do. We became acquainted in my formative years of high school, but it wasn't until college that she sharpened her skills of pride and arrogance. While attending Brigham Young University, my ego flourished in the ballet program (dance is a fertile breeding ground for the ego with so much emphasis placed on the physical body). Ballet students were required to maintain a certain weight in order to stay in the program. Existing on popcorn and grapefruit as my main diet, I was able to maintain a weight of ninety-eight pounds. Dance was an excuse to drive my body to extremes, even if it resulted in injury, for perfection was the ultimate goal of my ego.

Once my dance career ended, I replaced it with a career in personal training and fitness, where my ego could again thrive. Ever the constant master, she was vigilant at requiring a standard of excellence beyond my reach. That way she could keep me crippled in a state of never feeling good enough. She fluctuated between admiring her physical appearance and then beating herself up because of it. Relentless and unforgiving, she was equally harsh on those around her. She had a cunning ability to elevate herself above others through judgment and condemnation.

The greatest role my ego played was that of the "single-mother victim." This was a role with lots of juicy drama attached to it. My ego stressed that no one had it harder than I did when it came to parenting. Self-doubt and fear of failure were the weapons it used when I compared my life to others. In order to survive, my clever ego squelched my spirit with feelings of inadequacy about my own capabilities as a mother. My ego hungered for others to see how hard I worked and sacrificed, for without their pity, my ego could not thrive.

It was at church one day that my ego met her demise. After the morning chant and meditation, the presiding monk stood and proceeded to speak: "Paramahansa Yogananda once said, 'Analyze your thoughts and see on what throne of consciousness your ego is seated. Are your thoughts centered around yourself or on others?'" The monk continued, "Man's attachment to matter keeps the soul confined to the body prison and prevents it from finding freedom in God." My ego was feeling hot and sweaty. *How often did I think about others? Was my soul confined to my body prison?*

I felt like the entire congregation was looking at me. Had he prepared this sermon just for me? Pandora's box was now open, and it was beginning to make sense. I was wrapped up in my own trials, life drama, and selfish pursuits. Perhaps my problems were the result of my own ego and ignorance. It was a humbling thought. The monk closed with these words by Yogananda: "Humbleness is magnetic and is a distributor of happiness and invites the all protecting wisdom of true friends and God." The seeds of humility had been planted that day on the fertile soil of my soul.

> "Just as the moon eclipses the sun... so the ego
> eclipses God's light."
> — The White Angels

As my spiritual transformation evolved and expanded, I began studying the teachings of ascended masters and saints. In my youth, I read the Old Testament, the New Testament, the Book of Mormon, and the Doctrine and Covenants. I considered myself a follower of Christ and his teachings, but now I was very interested in the teachings of Krishna and Buddha. They all share the same message of love and compassion. One night after meditation, I had a question for the White Angels.

> "Ascended masters are a direct link from God to humankind. They have lived many incarnations and through great discipline and grace have discovered the truths of the universe. All ascended masters are avatars—physical manifestations of God. Jesus Christ, Buddha, and Krishna are all examples of ascended masters. Ascended masters have focused all of their intention on God for multiple lifetimes and choose to incarnate with the life mission of the teacher. Through their example and words, they are a beacon of light to others.

> "Great masters leave behind their energy in the places they walked upon the earth. This is why

many follow the footsteps of these divine masters. Great masters also leave behind their energy in their words. This is true for any of the holy scriptures. When one reads these words, ask the divine master to help with clear understanding. Ask that the message be delivered to you as it was intended. This will help eliminate any misinterpretation of the meaning behind their words.

"Ascended masters remain always near to help us along our path. Never hesitate to ask them directly for answers to your questions. No one is too unworthy to access the Divine. It is a law of the universe. Ask and you shall receive."
— The White Angels

It has been said that "Prayer is when you talk to God; meditation is when you listen to God." Meditation was my direct connection with God. I started practicing meditation regularly for longer periods of time. Some days I could not get past the mindless chatter in my head that kept me from going deeper. My mind would review my to-do list for the day or whatever activity I had planned after meditation. Eventually and with practice, I began to listen to the stillness that lies beyond the mind. Some call this being in the vortex, others call it a state of void or zero. I call this deep state of meditation "The God Zone."

The God Zone is where there are no restrictions or limitations and all things are possible. It is the realm of infinite possibilities. It is where time and space disappear. It is a vortex of energy where the universal sound of OM hums in the background and the divine flow of God vibration consumes the conscious mind until there is no more identity with the self. It brings such a state of peace that the breath and the heartbeat slow until body awareness disappears. A vibrant indigo blue emerges just behind closed eyes, eventually turning into a golden light as bright as the sun. This light permeates every cell in the body, raising one's own vibration. In my experience, the God Zone is where angels fly and alchemy begins.

"As a result of meditation, new channels are formed in the brain, new thought currents are generated, and new brain cells are formed." —Swami Vishnudevananda

"There is another world only to be discovered through meditation and prayer. Close the eyes and still the mind... listen to God's words. Hear God in the stillness, through the sound of OM. Your hearts beat to the sound of OM, the sound of unconditional love. It is in this stillness that you will find God. Perseverance, trust, and a pure heart are the tools of devotion that pave the road to God."
— The White Angels

When I was ready to progress further on my spiritual path, the angels opened the doors of opportunity for me to step into a world of wisdom and spiritual discipline. It was through a series of synchronicities that my husband Joe was transferred to the island Nassau, New Providence, Bahamas. The news was bittersweet. I couldn't imagine moving so far away from family and friends, but I trusted that God had a plan.

It wasn't difficult adjusting to the Bahamian lifestyle. It helped that our fifteenth-floor apartment overlooked the stunning crystal blue ocean. Every morning I was greeted by a spectacular sunrise that filled the sky with vibrant orange, pink, and purple, and every evening was a repeat performance. There is an old Bahamian saying that when God was done painting the sunrise, he dipped his brush in the Caribbean Sea. As much as I missed my family and friends, the beauty of the island soon had me captivated.

One day while exploring the island, I discovered a jewel located just across the Nassau Harbor. It sparkled amid the large cruise ships that monopolized the harbor, shining with the words SIVANADA ASHRAM YOGA RETREAT, aptly located on Paradise Island. An ashram is a secluded place for retreat, used for religious purposes or instruction in Hinduism, founded on the principals of yoga. As a yoga instructor, it had been a dream of mine to one day visit an ashram, and for some reason I thought that trip would lead me to India. To my surprise and delight (and I am sure a little divine intervention), I found that I was now living just a few miles away from one.

The founder of the ashram, Swami Vishnudevananda, once said, "Only in ashrams can students really start on the spiritual path, do intense *sadhana*, and get into the vibration." Swami Vishnudevananda was a disciple of Swami Sivananda. He was instructed by Sivananda to leave India, go to the West, and spread the teachings of yoga. In 1969 he established the True World Order and conducted the first yoga teachers training course (TTC) designed to teach the yogic disciplines. It was his goal to train future leaders, of which he said, "It is of vital importance that leaders have inner vision and inner peace. Not until men have this inner peace can they hope to establish global peace."

I couldn't wait to visit the ashram. I found that the only access to the ashram was by a small boat the locals nicknamed "the yoga boat." Three days a week, I caught the first boat of the day at 7:30 a.m., arriving just in time for the 8:00 a.m. yoga class. It was an invigorating way to start the morning with the spray of the ocean mist in my face and the cool Bahamian breeze blowing through my hair. Omkar, the captain of the tiny vessel, was always dressed in white yoga pants, a yellow Sivananda t-shirt, and bare feet. When we arrived at the small dock, a yellow archway with the words SIVANANDA ASHRAM YOGA RETREAT beckoned us to enter.

Students were setting up their yoga mats on a large deck overlooking the Nassau Harbor.

I made my way to the back platform located on the opposite side of the ashram. This was where the intermediate/advanced class was taught and it had a stunning view of the Atlantic Ocean. On windy days, the sound of the ocean would drown out the voice of the teacher, so I had to pay close attention to his instructions. I looked forward to the end of class when we lay on our mats and relaxed in *savasana* (corpse pose). The kitchen was located next to the ocean-facing platform and a batch of chocolate chip cookies was made fresh every morning. With the sweet smell of cookies and the calming sound of the ocean waves, it was heaven on earth.

When Joe announced that he was being transferred back to San Diego, my heart sank. I wasn't ready to leave the island and, more importantly, the ashram. It had become my home away from home. In addition, Joe and I were leaving behind many dear friends who had become family to us. I vowed to one day return and complete the teacher-training certification. The following is an entry from my daily journal at the time:

"Moving back to San Diego has been an adjustment. I miss the Bahamas, and in all honesty, I was not ready to leave. I had hoped to be there a few more years, but God has a plan. It has only been a few months since we left the island, but Joe and I have decided it is a good time for me to return and complete the TTC training. I look forward to living at the ashram and growing in my spiritual practice. I anticipate this experience will be life changing. Sometimes, I wish I could read ahead in this journal to see what is in front of me. For now, I must be patient and trust that all is revealed in God's time."

Before I knew it, I was headed back to the Bahamas, this time with a commitment to immerse myself in ashram living. Flying over the azure blue Caribbean Sea felt familiar. I was reflective as I looked out of the airplane window and thought about the month ahead. The taxi driver at the airport knew exactly where the "yoga boat" was located. He raced from one roundabout to another until we were in downtown Nassau. Tourists lined the streets in their brightly colored attire, stopping at the busy straw market to buy handmade baskets and woodcarvings. The taxi driver dropped me off at the dock with my oversized suitcase just in time to find Omkar pulling up the yoga to the dock. His smile and warm greeting made me feel as though I had never left.

The first day at the ashram was teacher-training orientation. My fellow classmates came from all over the world—Europe, South America, Asia, the Middle East, Canada, and the United States. During orientation, I sat next to a girl named Christie who was dressed in all white. She had an angelic face with a certain charisma that seemed innocent yet provocative. The students listened as our teachers explained the rules and regulations and what we could expect for the month ahead. They reiterated the program's policy of no caffeine, no alcohol, no smoking, and no sex during the month of TTC. Panic set in at the thought of no coffee or red wine, but I was committed.

The morning bell rang each day at 5:30 a.m. and *Manu* (vow of silence) was kept by all to ensure a reverent atmosphere. Satsang, a gathering of spiritual people (literally, "gathering together for the truth") began at 6:00 a.m. I quietly made my way to the garden platform and joined the others for meditation. "Close your eyes, and sit up tall like a mountain," the Swami began. There were more than 100 in attendance during satsang, and yet at that moment you could hear a pin drop. Focusing on my breath I settled into meditation, detaching from what was going on around me. Deep peace flooded my mind and body, and I was filled with an overwhelming sense of gratitude knowing I was where God wanted me to be.

The morning meditation was followed by *Kirtan* (devotional singing and chanting) and then an hour of lecture by a guest speaker. Following satsang, the teacher-training students engaged in two hours of advanced *asana* (yoga postures) practice. I placed my mat close to the stage so I had a bird's-eye view of the teachers. Christie set her mat up next to mine. Dressed in all white, she looked like a Hindu goddess. As the days progressed, we continued to take class next to each other and became good friends. Her level of skill far surpassed mine, which I found to my advantage as she patiently agreed to spot my headstands and futile attempts at the scorpion and peacock poses.

Two vegetarian meals were served each day at 10:00 a.m. and 6:00 p.m.—piping hot trays of lentil stew, daal, and curry were served along with fresh vegetables and fruits. I indulged in homemade bread, almond butter, and jam as a reward for the rigor of the morning activities. Picnic tables were placed on the sand, providing a million-dollar ocean view while we savored our delicious food. We could see the Atlantis Paradise Island Resort off to the right in the distance. The grand nautical towers were such a contrast to the simplicity of the ashram. Looming over the ocean, I imagined Atlantis symbolizing the material world, while the Sivananda Ashram represented the spiritual world.

Every TTC student was assigned one hour of service (karma yoga) each day. Fortunately, my previous time at the ashram had given me an advantage. Instead of washing dirty dishes, I was given the opportunity to work with Lalita Devi, the director of the well-being center and a clinical ayurvedic specialist. Ayurveda (the science of life) is a 5,000-year-old system of healing that originated in India. Before we moved back to San Diego, I visited Lalita for an ayurvedic consultation, where she determined my *dosha* (bio-elements) and created a program for my optimal health. It had been many months since I had last seen her, but we had developed a friendship and a mutual admiration for the science of ayurveda.

After completing my karma yoga hour, I had a fifteen-minute break before class to grab my books and head to the main temple for yoga philosophy. The schedule was tight and required discipline and dedication. The following is an entry in my daily journal:

"I literally run from class to class! The schedule is so intense and there is so much to learn, I feel overwhelmed. We are required to memorize the chants in Sanskrit, which is so foreign to me. Despite the pace, I am enjoying every precious moment. Even my little tent hut is starting to feel like home. Today I had a killer headache and I am sure it is because I am detoxing from alcohol and caffeine. I feel truly blessed to be here and have this experience."

Yoga philosophy was taught in the main temple, where pictures of Swami Sivananda and Swami Vishnudevananda hung on the walls. Statues of Hindu deities lovingly covered with flower leis stood on the main platform. Our teacher, "Swami B," sat in sukhasana (legs crossed) with his long orange robes gathered around his feet, waiting patiently for the students to enter the temple. Each class began as we collectively chanted the *Dhyana Slokas* (opening prayer). Swami B's voice was soft and gentle and his humor came at just the right time, rescuing us from information overload. In yoga philosophy, we learned about the four paths of yoga that include Karma yoga, Bhakti yoga, Raja yoga, and Jnana yoga.

Bhagavad Gita was the next class on the daily schedule. Bhagavad Gita literally translates to "the song of God," and the entire scripture takes place on a battlefield. It is a conversation between Krishna, the divine teacher, and Arjuna, the disciple. Shankar, our teacher, began each class chanting the verses of the Bhagavad Gita. Shankar once served in the Israeli army and he could not hide his good looks and masculinity behind the traditional yellow robes of a *Brahmachari* (a student of the Vedas). His muscular exterior was a contrast to his kind and gentle interior. He truly was a man of God, but that didn't keep the female population from swooning.

Following the Bhagavad Gita class, we had two more hours of asana practice, then dinner and evening satsang. I had one free hour a day where I managed to squeeze in a shower or do laundry. Satsang ended at 10:00 p.m., and everyone quietly made their way to their tent for lights out by 11:00 p.m. By the end of the first week, I wasn't sure what hit me. I had done yoga for the past fifteen years, but I had no idea the discipline required to live at an ashram. The pace was exhausting. Each night as I climbed into my little tent, I laid my head on the stiff foam pillow, and before I knew it the 5:30 a.m. bell was ringing.

Feeling restless one evening during satsang, I yearned to go back to my tent and call Joe. It had been almost two weeks, and I needed to hear his voice. What was he doing tonight? My mind wandered off as I pictured him curled up by the fireplace reading a book, surrounded by dogs and cats. The evening guest speaker stood and introduced himself as Dr. Amit Goswami. He was short, casually dressed, wearing a green fishing cap, and spoke with a strong Indian accent. Dr. Goswami had recently written a book titled *Quantum Creativity* and was here for the week to lecture on the topic. He looked vaguely familiar, and I racked my brain to figure out why. He then revealed he had participated in a film called *What the Bleep Do We Know?!*, one of my favorite new-age movies. Daydreaming took a back seat to Dr. Goswami's lecture, and as the hour came and went, I hung onto his every word. To my surprise, visions of sitting by the fireplace with Joe had been replaced with quantum physics.

I wanted to learn more about quantum physics, so the next day I decided to give up my only free hour to sit in on Dr. Goswami's lecture. I found him surrounded by a small group of eight people discussing the principals of non-locality and tangled hierarchy. I joined the group and listened intently.

"You wanna be creative? Searching for something, some field of exploration that matches your dharma," he said. "Expect the unexpected events of synchronicity will bring you the shoe that fits."

This piqued my interest. I knew about synchronicity; the very fact that I was sitting in this lecture was a fine example of it. His words resonated at such a deep level that I crashed the class every day that week.

We had most of the day free on Saturdays, and most students dedicated the day to doing homework and taking much-needed naps. My birthday fell on the third Saturday, and to celebrate I scheduled a massage at the wellness center. In addition, I booked an appointment with the tantric priest to have my Vedic astrology chart read. A big fan of astrology, I was familiar with Chinese and Western astrology, but Vedic astrology was new to me. Vedic astrology, or Jyotisha, means "light, heavenly body" in Sanskrit. After my ayurvedic massage, I ventured to a small hut at the edge of the ashram that had a stunning view of the harbor. There, I was greeted at the door by the tantric priest.

His full title displayed on the desk read, "Tantric Priest,

Vedic Astrologer, Hatha Yoga Teacher, and Puja and Homa Specialist." He was a short man, dressed in yellow robes and leather sandals. His office was small but bright with pictures of Hindu deities on the walls. With a large smile and broken English, he invited me in and asked me to sit as he pointed to a bamboo-folding chair. Next to the chair was a wooden table covered with small shells and crystals. The priest sat next to me and began strategically moving the shells and crystals around on a chalk grid that had been drawn on the table. Once the shells and crystals were in place, he began talking with his heavy Indian accent. Pen and paper in hand, I scribbled as fast as he spoke.

"In two years, you will start a new profession in the healing arts. You must paint your meditation room white and hang pictures of deities on the wall for blessings." He continued to move shells and crystals around, and with each pause I waited for the next enlightened message. He told me things about my husband and daughters that were very insightful, things that eventually came to pass. When the reading was complete, I thanked the priest and headed to my tent for a much-needed nap, my head spinning with messages of my future. *Healing arts... What could that be?* I wondered to myself.

The month was up, and my time at the ashram was coming to an end. The experience was spiritual alchemy for me, a personal transformation through meditation, education, and soul searching. My last journal entry reflected this.

"I am leaving the ashram today. Last night was graduation and I received my spiritual name, OmKari. I was told it means the trinity of goddesses: Lakshmi, Saraswati, and

Durga. This has been a life changing experience for me. The TTC program caused me to push myself physically, mentally, emotionally, and spiritually. I came expecting to get clarity, and I received so much more. I have discovered that my spiritual practice (sadhana) is vitally important to me. In order to continue to grow into the person I want to be, I cannot compromise my sadhana. I must live yoga, not just practice yoga. Swami Sivananda said, "The highest yoga is to bear insult, bear injury." His message of Serve-Love-Give-Purify-Meditate-Realize will be my lifelong pursuit.

Chapter 10

Angels and Enlightenment

THERON

"Continue to search for knowledge. God can work miracles upon your faith. All things are possible."

"The happiness that comes from the pleasures of the world is but a minute reflection of the infinite bliss that comes from within your very own self."
—Amma (Mata Amritanandamayi Devi)

It had been four months since I left the ashram.

Returning to San Diego after such a transformation was an adjustment. I was different. I yearned for the sounds and smells of the ashram, the yogis and their bright smiles and orange robes. I missed the morning and evening satsungs filled with meditation and chanting. Now that I was back home, I began a daily practice of chanting and meditation. My personal practice brought me clarity and direction, but I felt alone and isolated on this path. I longed for the comradery and unity the ashram offered.

Surfing the Internet one night, I saw a post on Facebook that said Amma (Mata Amritanandamayi) was coming to Los Angeles. It was just four days away, and I wasn't sure if tickets were still available, but I knew I had to attend. As luck would have it, there were still a few tickets left—however, all accommodations were sold out. None of the hotels in the area were vacant, so I ended up staying in Irvine some forty miles away. I knew that I needed to attend this conference at all costs, so driving eighty miles a day to see "the Hugging Saint" was a sacrifice I was willing to make.

Amma means "Mother," as she is known by her followers. As a young child, Amma showed extraordinary compassion to those around her. With the call to follow God instead of marrying, as was the tradition in India, Amma began a worldwide foundation that engages in spiritual and charitable activities. She began hugging those that came to her with their troubles as a way to show them love and compassion. Thirty years later, Amma has embraced more than 33 million people throughout the world. Hugging people has become her form of giving to others, which is referred to as *Darshana* (act of seeing) in Hinduism. She continues to do so to this day, and Amma has been known to give Darshana for more than twenty continuous hours without rest.

The retreat was held at the Hilton Los Angeles Airport with three full days of events that included meditation, devotional singing, spiritual teachings, yoga, workshops, lectures, Kirtan (chanting), and *Pujas* (prayer ritual). Vegetarian meals were included as part of the registration fee, and the last meal was personally served by Amma. My *mala* beads (traditionally used for counting during mantra meditations) were packed, and I was ready to immerse myself in the spirit of love and compassion for the weekend.

The day began early with a 7:00 a.m. yoga class followed by meditation and Kirtan. The Sanskrit chants reminded me of my days at the Sivananda Ashram and the early morning satsang. The Hilton ballroom was certainly missing the fresh Bahamian air and soothing sounds of the ocean in the background. Although the ballroom was a far cry from the beauty of the ashram, the room was filled with a powerful vibration and energy given off by the hundreds of participants there for this auspicious weekend. I was definitely getting my yoga fix.

I took a seat in the center of the ballroom about five rows back from the front stage. To the left of me sat a gentleman who introduced himself as Martin. I asked Martin where his accent was from, and he told me he was originally from Prague but was currently residing in Malibu. This was also Martin's first experience seeing Amma. Martin was new on the spiritual path and to my delight had recently visited Paramahansa Yogananda's Lake Shrine Temple where he was participating in weekly group meditations. I remembered my time at the Lake Shrine Temple in Pacific Palisades, where I experienced my first attempts at meditation.

Sitting on the opposite side of me was woman named Joanna. Joanna lived in Montana on a ranch with her husband and had attended many of Amma's American retreats. She was a physic medium and appeared very earthy and grounded. Joanna, Martin, and I engaged in stimulating conversation, sharing stories and getting acquainted while we waited for Amma's arrival.

When Amma arrived, she was dressed in a beautiful white sari with her dark hair pulled back in a bun. An entourage greeted her by placing pink and white flower leis around her neck while throwing rose petals at her feet. Amma gave off an air of unconditional love to all as she entered the room. Her smile was warm and inviting. Martin turned to me and said, "Can you see that?" commenting on the aura that surrounded her. I couldn't see anything, but apparently Amma had a rainbow aura that left him in awe.

Joanna was too busy commenting on the angels that surrounded Amma to hear Martin's comment. "Archangel Michael and his Band of Mercy are here protecting her. Look at the gentleman standing beside Amma." She pointed to a young, tall blond man standing next to Amma. He was dressed in all black with a blue tie. "He is one of Archangel Michael's Band of Mercy," she continued. Archangel Michael was not the only angel in the room; there were hundreds of angels, including everyone's guardian angels. I knew there was something special about Amma, something saintly and divine.

Amma took her seat on the stage, and the audience became very quiet. She spoke a few words to us, and then we went into a long period of meditation. Following meditation, Amma lead us in Kirtan. The Sanskrit words were displayed on a wide screen above the stage so we could follow along while musicians played the sitar and percussion instruments. At times Amma seemed as if she was lost in the chant, her eyes closed and her head tilted back as she called the name of Rama. The music was intoxicating, and I soon felt lost in the rich sounds of ancient India as we chanted our devotion.

Once satsang ended, Amma stood to take a seat in a large chair that looked fit for a queen. She was ready to give Darshana to the group. We lined up according to the number we were given at the door and waited for our turn to receive a divine hug. I watched as each individual took their turn kneeling in front of Amma. She lovingly embraced them to her chest. I could see tears in their eyes and a look of overwhelming joy radiating from their faces. When they walked away, they looked as if a transformation had taken place within them. I wondered how I would feel in the arms of this Indian saint.

Next in line, I was instructed by her assistant to kneel on the floor while I waited my turn. I could see Amma's face as she embraced the person in front of me. She wore a diamond and gold nose ring and a bindi (a red dot considered the sacred symbol of the cosmos in its unmanifested state) on the center of her forehead. Amma wore two mala bracelets on each wrist made from the traditional sandalwood, *rudraksha* beads, and a strand of beads around her neck. Her eyes were closed as she rocked the grown man back and forth as if she was holding a small child to her chest. She released her gentle grip and the gentleman reluctantly turned away from her. Tears streamed down his face, and he looked like as if he had just had an out-of-body experience.

I knelt in front of Amma and placed my hands on the arms of the large chair she was sitting in. We had been instructed not to touch her while she hugged us. She gently grabbed my face and pulled it into her chest, placing the side of my face against her shoulder. I felt the warmth of her body radiating against me, my heart connecting with hers. I felt like I was drowning in her love. I could hear her softly chanting as she held me tight. My mind was flooded with the thought of the divine mother and I repeated the words "Divine mother, my divine mother" in my head.

After a few minutes, Amma looked at me and dabbed sandalwood paste on my forehead (at my third eye). Then she held me close to her one more time. I did not want this all-consuming bliss to end. Her release was bittersweet, and I longed for more. Slowly I stood, and as I turned away, I knew for myself what it was like to be transformed by her love. It was as if, for a brief moment, time stood still and I was fully connected to the consciousness behind the universe. I was floating in the fragrance of unconditional love.

"Like a drop of water that falls into the sea and merges in its vast expansiveness, the devotee dives into the ocean of bliss as he offers himself to existence. Drowning in the ocean of love, he lives always in love. Fully consumed by divine love, his individual existence is lost, for he has merged with the totality of love. He becomes an offering of love to his Lord. In that state of pure love, all fear, all worries, all attachments, and all sorrows disappear." —Amma

Amma is considered to be an enlightened being. The

qualities of an enlightened being include humility, love, peace, patience, mindfulness, and forgiveness. An enlightened being remains in constant communication with the Divine while interacting with others on this earthly plane. Describing her journey to enlightenment, Amma recounts: "From that day onwards I could see nothing as different from my own Formless Self wherein the entire universe exists as a tiny bubble..."

Regarding enlightenment, Swami Vishnudevanada wrote in his book *Meditations and Mantras*, "Cosmic consciousness is an inherent, natural faculty of all men and women. Training and discipline are necessary to awaken the consciousness. It is already present in man. It is inactive or non-functioning in the majority of human beings on account of the force of *Avidya* or ignorance."

To achieve enlightenment and awaken our consciousness, our hearts must be freed from all that is not love. This can be achieved through forgiveness of oneself and others. Forgiveness is essential to our happiness. The White Angels tell me that **"Forgiveness is the key that unlocks the universe."** Jesus was a perfect example of this when on the cross he said, "Father, forgive them, for they know not what they do" (Luke 23:24).

> "We do not use the term forgiveness as you call it. Too many individuals are attached to this word through religious convictions and do not understand the principle. One must see themselves in others to use this principle fully. If hearts are pure and vibrations are high, there is never a need to harm another in any way, mentally with thoughts or physically through actions. To see God in others is

to live in the light. Would one hurt God? Then why do harm to another?

"Holding onto negative feelings for others creates havoc in one's life. These feelings cause disease in the body and unhappiness. Let go and free your heart from the burden of negative emotions. They do not come from God. Release yourself from such bondage and fill your heart with love for yourself and others. Ask God and the angels for help in all matters. Everything is possible with love; it is the universal healer. Clear your heart and mind from negativity as you would clear your home from debris. Throw out all that does not serve you and burn it in the fire of love.

"Love is the ultimate balm of salvation. Love is forgiveness, it encompasses all that is good. Loving one another as oneself is the universal law of unity. It is for this purpose the universe was created, from love and with love. Cleanse yourself with love, heal with love, and purify with love. Love is not an action but an opening."
— The White Angels

Amma radiates pure cosmic consciousness and bliss to all she meets through the vibration of enlightenment. I was fortunate to experience this vibration for myself as she embraced me in her arms. Enlightenment is not exclusive to the sages of India and prophets of old, but for all that seek it. It is our birthright as children of God.

"Enlightenment is the goal of all who come to Earth. It is the path that leads one back to Source. The path to enlightenment is extremely difficult and requires great discipline to achieve. It cannot be attained without a physical body (in the astral

or causal world), but must be actualized while in a physical incarnation. Enlightenment is the purpose of all collective lifetimes. It requires a pure heart and constant focus. It is the eye of the needle. Reaching the state of enlightenment ends the cycle of physical incarnations. The soul is then free. Unconditional love acquired by complete forgiveness and humility opens the door to enlightenment."
— The White Angels

As Lao Tzu says, "Returning to the root is called stillness: stillness is called return to life, return to life is called the constant; knowing the constant is called enlightenment."

How does enlightenment differ from ascension? In her book *Angel Answers*, Diana Cooper writes, "Enlightenment is a state of being... ascension is a state of doing." Diana's definition of ascension is simply "raising your frequency to a higher level." The White Angels give the following message about ascension:

"Forgiveness is the first step on the ladder of ascension."
— The White Angels

While enlightenment is the goal of all who come to earth, ascension is the ladder that takes us there. We must continuously strive to raise our vibration to reach the goal of enlightenment or constant communication with the Divine.

"Ascension is like climbing a ladder: you must take it one step at a time. All of creation is on a path of ascension—plants, animals, humankind, and your planet. Everything must ascend to transform, nothing stays the same. A shift to spiritual

enlightenment and ascension of your planet has
begun. God is sending universal help in the form of
angels and other celestial beings to help with this
process. Truth and light will be revealed like never
before.

"One has only to ask God and the angels for divine
assistance in sending love and light to your planet
and all inhabitants to aid in the ascension process.
Ask and it shall be given. We rejoice in your asking
so that we many help. You are not alone; you are
one with all. God loves you and the angels love
you."
— The White Angels

Spiritual discipline and devotion are steps on the ladder
of ascension leading to enlightenment. In the ashram, this
is called sadhana (spiritual practice). We were taught that
sadhana was the most important duty of the day and must be
approached with a sincere attitude along with an openness
to learn. Perseverance, dedication, and consistency are most
beneficial in obtaining a spiritual practice; however, God
gives all of his children an A+ for all their efforts.

Chapter 11

Discovering Your Life's Purpose

HELIXX

"Follow the path of light, it will lead you to your
true purpose, your mission on earth."

"Decide the nature of your true task—your mission in
life. Endeavor to make yourself what you should be and
what you want to be. Your ultimate purpose is to find your
way back to God, but you also have a task to perform in the
outer world." —Paramahansa Yogananda

Have you ever asked the questions, *Why am I here?* and *What
is the purpose of my life?* If you have, you are not alone. Humankind

has been searching for the answer to these questions since the beginning of time. Many of my clients come seeking guidance from their angels about their life's purpose. They want a quick and easy answer, but the angels advise me to first help them align with who they are as a soul. They must recognize that they are a soul, a spark of God, before they can step onto their path and discover their true life's purpose.

> "Each of you are a spark of light from Source. Each spark is as individual as a snowflake. The soul is born of God and eventually returns to God. The soul journey is vast and expansive with the intent to discover, co-create, and expand. Each soul spark is born into a physical body, but the veil of knowledge masks your true identity causing you to forget you are a spark of God, a powerful co-creator with the Divine.
>
> "The soul's journey is a difficult one filled with many lessons. Each lesson is determined by the soul so that it might reach its full potential and once again return to God. If the soul does not learn the lesson, it will be repeated with more difficulty in the next life. This is the law of Karma.
>
> "The most important lesson for every soul is that of forgiveness and unconditional love for all things. To move beyond the wheel of Karma, the soul must once again see the spark of God in itself and others. This is the law of unity. When all lessons are learned, the soul ascends the ladder of knowledge and wisdom until the earth school is complete and it need not return. The soul then graduates to a higher dimension where expansion continues."
> — The White Angels

I discovered my life's purpose later in life. I did not seek it; however, when I was ready, it found me. It was more like a calling. Looking back, I see now that I was guided to the healing-arts path spoken of in my astrology reading at the Sivananda Ashram. Entering the ashram was the first step onto my path. Since then, by following my heart and the promptings of the angels, a magical world has unfolded before me.

"Life is your purpose. To live life fully in every moment is your purpose. To love yourself and others unconditionally is your purpose. To seek truth, wisdom, and knowledge is your purpose. To allow yourself to be who you are without judgement is your purpose. You do not need to find your purpose or spend a lifetime seeking your purpose. It will find you when you are ready to live as you agreed to live.

"It is not necessary to strive for greatness. Greatness will come when you are ready to receive it. Some find greatness through living a humble life while others are called to be leaders and teachers of men. When you align with your true self, your path will unfold before you. You will know when it is right. You will feel it in your heart. It is who you are and were meant to be in the beginning. Do not seek it, it will come.

"Ask God and the angels to light your path, and then trust. You are all unique children of God and each given gifts to share for the benefit of others. When you are ready, your gift will be made known unto you."
— The White Angels

I believe we determine our life's purpose or life's mission prior to incarnating on earth. We make the decision based upon our spiritual growth and the karmic lessons we need to learn, and it is our guardian angel that holds the blueprint to our life's purpose. Our guardian angels are with us when we determine what our purpose will be, and they lovingly agree to guide us to that calling. It is up to us to tune into their whispers and follow that guidance. As the White Angels tell us, **"When you align with your true self, your path will unfold before you. You will know when it is right; you will feel it in your heart."**

How do we align with our true selves? I believe it begins by living a life of authenticity. Are you being true to yourself? Does your life bring you happiness and joy or frustration and disappointment? When we make decisions based on love instead of fear, our life's purpose begins to unfold before us. Love is the ability to trust that God knows what is best for you and fear is the need to control what you cannot.

I was once told to "think from your heart, not your head." We possess all of the answers we need; however, we must go within to find them. This is not always easy, but if you ask your angels for help, they will guide you. Know that the angels are working behind the scenes on your behalf to light your path. Be patient and trust your intuition. Trust that there is a divine plan for your life, and understand that all will be revealed in divine timing.

> "Trust is the ability to 'let go and let God,' knowing fully in your heart that all will be done for your greatest and highest good. Did not God create you? How then can you not trust that he knows what is best for his child? We understand this is not easy. It is difficult for some to relinquish what they perceive to be control of their life or any given situation. This is delusion. Trust that God will take care of all things in divine timing.

"Divine timing is never your timing. Be patient
in the knowing that all will be revealed in time.
Sometimes what you think best for your life is
counter-productive to your mission or purpose.
Trust that God knows what is best for you, and then
release your worries, fears, and doubts to him. God
is benevolent and only wants for your happiness and
well-being. In that you must trust."
— The White Angels

The following exercise has helped me when I needed to trust that all would work out in God's timing:

Visualize placing your questions, concerns, and problems in a bubble, and send them to heaven for a blessing. Ask God to shine light on the contents of the bubble and then fully release it. Trust that it is in God's hands and let go. Now call in Archangel Uriel to shine his light upon your life. He will illuminate your path, but it is up to you to take the necessary steps required to follow that path. Ask the angels to help you trust and have faith that all will work out in divine order. Thank God and the angels for their help, and trust that all will work out for your greatest and highest good.

I believe we all have individual callings to fulfill on earth, but our true life's purpose is to learn to love unconditionally. It is our individual and collective life lesson as children of God. Love God and love your neighbor as yourself; it is as simple as that. Yet, in our ignorance we place the small self, our ego, before others, and for that we suffer unnecessarily. Living a life filled with unconditional love requires our ego to surrender to our higher self, our soul. It requires conscious commitment to live in the present moment with full awareness of our every thought, word, and action. When you live in the vibration of love, you discover that love is the elixir for all of life's ailments. Love heals all wounds.

"There is no greater message than love. It is the most powerful force and vibration in the cosmos. By seeking love first, one will discover all the riches in the universe. God's blessings flow in abundance to the heart of one who loves unconditionally. An abundant life is a life filled with love. No material wealth can provide happiness without it. No amount of worldly power can provide happiness without it.

"We do not speak of love as it is commonly known to you. We speak of an unconditional love that comes from God. One cannot love purely if conditions are attached. Conditions and attachments are rooted in selfishness originating from fear. Fear is the opposite of love; it is a destructive force. It is necessary in this lifetime to conquer your fears. Ask God and the angels for help in conquering your fears. Ask God daily to bless you with love and light. Ask God daily to bless others with love and light. Ask God daily to bless your planet with love and light. And so it is."
— The White Angels

When you vibrate at the frequency of love, your life purpose becomes clear. You begin manifesting by the law of attraction those desires that come from your heart. The universe will bring people and opportunities to you that match the frequency of your desires, and it is only a matter of time before your life's purpose unfolds miraculously before you. When you stay in the vibration of love, you witness miracles on a daily basis and begin to see your life as one big miracle.

"Miracles are not an unusual occurrence in the cosmos. They are nature's law in action, but you do not see it this way. These laws are not familiar to many of you so you perceive it to be a miraculous event. Miracles as you understand them are happening all of the time, all around you. You must open your spiritual awareness to witness them.

"There are many miracles that you take for granted because you are familiar with the law. The miracle of life and birth. The miracle of a tiny seedling growing into a tall tree. The miracle of the sunrise and sunset each day. The miracle of the planets orbiting around the sun in exact precision. When one begins to appreciate the miracles that appear daily and without effort, one then opens to experiencing miracles on a grander level.

"Appreciation and gratitude are the codes that activate the law of attraction, therefore if you want to see more miracles in your life, you must be grateful for the daily miracles around you. Eventually you will begin to see your own life as one big miracle. You will begin to experience miraculous things on a daily basis. You will understand that miracles are not saved only for the saints and rishis but for all of God's children."
— The White Angels

Appreciating the life you have been given and waking each day in gratitude is like stepping onto the yellow brick road that leads to your true purpose. Aligning with who you really are by seeing the Divine in all things continues you down that road until one day you wake up and it has found you. It is your divine birthright to fulfill your calling, your mission, and purpose here on earth. Your guardian angel is here to help you along the way.

Close your eyes and ask yourself the following question: "If money were no object, what would I be doing?" Now tune into your heart and meditate for a moment on the answer. Once the answer comes to you, write it down, and do not limit yourself. Your list may take up two pages or it may be a simple sentence. Be careful not to overthink this question; it should come from your heart, not your head. You should feel passionate about the answer on a soul level. It should excite you and make you feel alive.

Remembering that you are a spark of God and your true purpose to see that spark in others is ultimately why you are here. However, we all have an individual mission to accomplish, a calling and purpose in life that feeds our soul. Follow your heart and ask your guardian angel to guide and direct you to that calling. Trust that all is in divine timing and your purpose will be revealed when you are ready. As the White Angels remind us, **"You do not need to find your purpose or spend a lifetime seeking your purpose. It will find you when you are ready to live as you agreed to live."**

Chapter 12
Angels and Energy

PHILIPA

"Stay in the light by keeping your thoughts positive.
Find your joy."

**"Love is the most powerful force and vibration in
the cosmos."**
—The White Angels

Everything in the universe is pure energy, from the sun
and moon, to the chair I am sitting on as I write this. Each
object vibrates at a different frequency, and this is referred
to as the vibrational rate. The law of the universe matches

the vibrational rate of all things, 'like attracts like.' Every thought we think and every word we speak carries with it a vibration. When we focus on positive thoughts, the law of attraction brings us positive experiences to match that vibration. In turn, negative thoughts will only bring more negativity and experiences you do not want.

"Every thought holds a vibration. There is a vibrating scale in the universe similar to a musical scale. The low notes are low vibrations and the high notes are high vibrations. Similarly, negative or low thoughts vibrate at a low vibration and positive thoughts vibrate at a high vibration. When you hit a note, you can hear the sound resonate in the air, and the same holds true for a thought. It fills the space around you and exists forever. Once created, the vibration of that thought is eternal.

"The lowest thought is that of fear and the opposing thought is love. There are many thoughts in between, each with its own vibration. It is impossible to jump from fear to love instantly, there is too big a gap, but one can jump from fear to hate, hate to anger, anger to sorrow, sorrow to remorse, remorse to hope, and so on.

"The most effective way to continue to raise your vibration is to focus on creating higher vibrating thoughts. Avoid becoming a slave to your thoughts and a complacent thinker. Choose your thoughts carefully and wisely. Meditate to create thoughtlessness and do away with mindless chatter that daily rages on in your head.

"Fill your mind with good books and inspiring words from others. Surround yourself with uplifting, high-vibrating individuals, events, and

places. When a negative thought comes to you, replace it immediately with the opposing positive thought. Your life is the total accumulation of every thought you think, so choose wisely."
—The White Angels

In his book *Messages from Water and Universe*, Dr. Masaru Emoto wrote about his study on the effect words have on water. He found that the combination of the words "love" and "gratitude" were the most powerful when used together. The vibration of these two words changed the water molecules into beautiful shapes resembling snowflakes. However, when he used the word "hate" the water molecules were distorted and ugly. As an explanation of this phenomena, Dr. Emoto wrote, "God created the concept of love; and as a representation of the receiving energy, He created the concept of gratitude. So, love is the active energy and gratitude is the passive receiving energy."

The highest frequency is the vibration of unconditional love. Unconditional love is the answer to all problems in this physical world. In any given moment, we have the choice to choose love over fear. When we make the choice to love, we raise our own vibration and the vibration of those around us. However, loving others is not always the easiest path to take. The White Angels tell me, **"The greatest challenge for humankind is to put away his selfishness and love his enemy."**

In her book *Convoluted Universe 5*, Dolores Cannon writes, "The original life force energy or source energy comes from the heart... once you are in that space, anything you think, feel, say, or do becomes reality."

"The most important lesson to teach others is how to raise their vibration. By raising your vibration, you are able to receive all good things from the universe. Higher vibrations lead to living a longer, happier, more satisfying life. You are here to experience unlimited joy in this life, and lower vibrations such as fear, anger, hate, and jealousy block joy. Fear is the lowest vibrating frequency and causes one to be out of alignment with God.

"The highest vibration is love. The vibration of love cleanses and purifies fear. Once the vibration of love is sustained fear is removed, for fear and love cannot exist at the same time. The key to having a peaceful happy world is in raising the vibration of each individual. It begins with the one. This will have a positive effect on all. Love is contagious, but it begins with the individual."
— The White Angels

The following is a list from the White Angels on how to raise our vibration.

1. There is nothing that can raise the vibration more quickly than reverently reciting the name of God.

2. Have unconditional love for yourself and others.

3. Practice meditation and prayer. One must quiet the mind to hear God, then pray from your heart in that silence.

4. Think loving thoughts. Control your thoughts and you control your destiny.

5. Sing songs that uplift one's soul and chant the universal sound of OM.

6. Serve others. When you serve others, you serve God.

7. Spend time in nature. Nature detoxifies and cleanses the spirit.

8. Exercise regularly. Bringing chi—the vital life force energy of the universe, present within every living thing—to the body through movement.

9. Drink water. Water is the ultimate purifier.

10. Eat high-vibrational foods. Oranges have the highest vibration of all foods.

There are many methods you can use to raise your vibration. Meditation and prayer are at the top of my list. Reiki is another way to raise your vibration. My introduction to Reiki came from a good friend of mine, Karl. It was divine timing as I had just returned to San Diego after my month at the Sivananda Ashram. My experience there had transformed my life, and I was wondering what was next on my spiritual path. Karl was a Reiki master and asked if I knew anything about Reiki. Thanks to my time at the ashram and my fascination with quantum physics, I was open to Reiki and the idea of energy healing.

Reiki is a natural energy-healing technique. It helps promote health and well-being in the body by working with chi (life energy). Reiki rebalances the flow of energy in and around the body to help return the body to a vibrant, positive state of health. Everything is made up of electromagnetic energy vibrating at different frequencies that correspond to sound and light. Therefore, *everything* can benefit from the healing power of Reiki.

The history of Reiki is quite recent, as it was discovered in 1920 by Mikao Usui. However, many believe it first originated in Tibet and has been in use for thousands of years. Dr. Usui received the powerful healing force he called Reiki on Mount Kurama in Japan, after fasting and meditating for twenty-one days. Mikao Usui became known as a sensei (teacher) and passed this technique onto a select few who studied with him in Japan. Reiki was eventually brought to Hawaii and New York, and from there it has flourished as an international method of energy healing.

I decided to enroll in the first level of Reiki training. In level one I was taught how to do Reiki on myself, my pets, and my plants. Fascinated, I continued on and took the level two certification. My instructors, Kathy and Bob, often use the mantra, "All Reiki all the time." I embraced the mantra by giving Reiki to my husband, family, friends, pet, plants, and food. I even use Reiki on inanimate objects like my car and computer. Realizing that I had a passion for Reiki, I committed to completing the Reiki master level.

Shortly after completing my Reiki training, Karl and I established PositiviChi, a company dedicated to bringing more positive energy to the world through Reiki. We began teaching Reiki classes and lecturing on the benefits of energy healing. During this time, I noticed my intuition deepening and clairvoyant abilities increasing. Because of Reiki and meditation, I was becoming sensitive to the unseen world around me. My angels had guided me to the healing-arts path that the Vedic astrologer at the ashram once foretold. As I stepped onto my life path, the universe arranged people, places, and things to manifest in my life. I felt a shift in my awareness and I knew that something magical was happening.

The first time I was visited by a guardian angel other than my own, I was giving my dad a Reiki treatment. Dad had developed a nasty case of the shingles virus and a red rash covered the left side of his head. This affected his eye and ear and he was in terrible pain. During the treatment, I placed my hands on his head and concentrated on bringing healing energy to his eye and ear. With my eyes closed, I suddenly saw a form through my third eye (the eye of wisdom). He introduced himself as Timothy, and told me he was my father's guardian angel.

Timothy told me Dad was suffering from shingles because of stress that was accumulating at work. He was now manifesting his stress physically in his head, he was "overthinking," using Timothy's words. Timothy was clothed in a white robe. He was holding scrolls in one hand and a golden caduceus staff—an ancient wand associated with healing—in the other. His manner was very gentle, and he reminded me of the quiet intellect of my father. I sat quietly communicating with Timothy while Dad slept through the Reiki treatment. Timothy told me what Dad needed to do in order to heal from his shingles and relieve the stress from work. I thanked him and asked him if I could contact him again on my father's behalf. He nodded yes, and then his shinning countenance was gone.

My dilemma was whether to tell Dad about his guardian angel. Growing up in the Mormon Church, we were taught Joseph Smith, the founder of the church, was visited by Angel Moroni. There are many accounts of angels in the Mormon scriptures; however, they appeared to the prophets and leaders, not the average folk, and especially not women. Healing is also reserved for men as it is believed healing powers are handed down from God through the Melchizedek Priesthood, restricted solely for the men in the church.

Receiving Reiki was a big enough step for Dad. He did not understand how it worked, but he didn't care as it relieved his pain and helped him sleep. I decided to have a discussion with Dad about his work and the effect stress was having on his health without mentioning his angel. Going forward, I called upon Timothy when I needed answers concerning my father's health and he always appeared during our Reiki sessions.

Angels began frequently appearing to me during Reiki treatments. One day I was working on a woman who had stomach cancer. She had recently been operated on and was now receiving chemotherapy treatments. When I placed my hands above her abdominal area, I knew that she had experienced emotional and physical trauma as a young girl. Her angel was lovingly by her side as I poured Reiki energy into the abdominal area. Most of the time my eyes are closed when I am giving a treatment, but I was guided to look up at this woman. She was fast asleep, her face radiating with the innocence of a beautiful young child while her guardian angel lovingly looked on. I knew that somehow the trauma she suffered as a young child was directly related to the pain she was suffering now as an adult, and I felt a sense of overwhelming compassion for her.

I will never forget the guardian angel who appeared looking very much like a wizard. I was giving Reiki to an elderly woman who complained of many aches and pains in her body. The moment I put my hands on her, I could see her guardian angel. He appeared dressed in a silver robe with a long gray beard. He told me this woman would not listen to his promptings. She suffered from TMJ (I didn't know this information prior to the treatment) and her body felt shut tight like a prison. There was no love going in or out.

Her guardian angel asked me to give her as much love and light as I could through the Reiki healing. Eventually I could feel her ice-cold interior starting to melt, and I could see his excitement as she filled up with love and light. A beautiful, peaceful calm radiated all over her face and she no longer looked like the same woman. It was as if I was looking at her through God's eyes and I could only see her beauty. When the treatment ended, she was very calm and happy. Her pain was gone. I was delighted and so was her guardian angel.

One of my most memorable moments came to me from a client that had recently had a heart transplant. When working with an organ transplant patient, I try to establish synergy between the newly transplanted organ and the receiving body. There must be a yin–yang of giving and receiving, otherwise the body might reject the organ. When I placed my hands on his chest, I could feel a disconnected energy. I visualized holding his new heart in my hands, sending healing energy and love to the heart. I asked the heart to accept this new body and release the energy connection it had to the previous body. I then asked the body to receive this new heart as its own and fully integrate it. My hands were hot and vibrating, and tears were rolling down my cheeks as I talked to the new heart. I could feel love and acceptance as I continued to send Reiki energy to his body. It was a beautiful experience, one that I will never forget.

The correlation between emotional blocks and disease has been documented by many well-known healers of our time. Even western medicine is beginning to see that there is some link between our repressed emotions and our health. I believe our emotions are the key to our health; this was evident with my father and his shingles diagnosis.

Reiki brings balance to the emotions by clearing negative energy that is blocked in the body. This energy is stored in the chakras, a system of energy centers, or vortexes within the body. These centers or vortexes vibrate at a specific frequency that corresponds to the systems in the body.

I was initially introduced to the chakra systems during my yoga training at the ashram. The Sanskrit word "chakra" means wheel, and I learned that when the chakras are healthy and open, the body functions properly. However, when a chakra is blocked, an imbalance is created in the body, and if left unattended, disease can manifest. Reiki helps to open and balance the chakras, keeping them healthy and preventing weakness in the body that could eventually manifest into physical illness or disease. Anodea Judith, author of *Eastern Body/Western Mind*, explains the chakra system as "a profound representation of the universe. Each of the seven levels represents such major areas of human life that they could fill volumes all by themselves."

Mikao Usui, the founder of Reiki, knew that our emotions were the key to our health and happiness. He became aware of the significance of this fact when many of his patients were healed only to return to him later with the same symptoms. Their physical healing was temporary because they continued to carry the emotional scars from living an unhappy life. Dr. Usui decided to create the Five Reiki Principles (*Gokai*) for his clients to help them maintain their health and live a happy life.

Five Reiki Principles (Gokai)

Just for today, I will not be angry.

Just for today, I will not worry.

Just for today, I will be grateful.

Just for today, I will do my duties.

Just for today, I will be kind to every living thing.

The human body is made up of 60 to 70 percent water. Keeping this in mind, Dr. Emoto's research on the effect that words have on the molecular structure of water is a key component to our health. In other words, our thoughts create our physical condition. Dr. Usui also knew the effects that words have on the body. He knew that if his patients recited positive affirmations daily, upon waking and sleeping, they would have a better chance of keeping their emotional and physical body healthy. By keeping our vibration high, through positive thinking and positive living, we will be an energetic match to the frequency of good health, happiness, and abundance.

Chapter 13

Cosmic Consciousness

REBEKA

*"View all as one. You are not separate.
You will be a great example to others."*

**"Rejoice in your oneness as a cosmic family and
share your gifts and blessings with one another.
Spread this message of love and unity to all and live
it fully and completely."**
— The White Angels

What if you were told you had one year to live? What is

the first thing that would come to your mind? Would you have a bucket list of desires yet to accomplish? Perhaps you would spend more time with your family or travel to distant places you have only dreamed of. I guarantee you would not stay in a job that made you unhappy. You probably wouldn't stay in a relationship that made you unhappy, either. With the thought of only one more precious year to live, you might be motivated to simplify your life or take a risk. What would you have to lose?

Now let me ask another question. What if you were told that you had many years to live, but this was your last life on the karmic wheel, your last incarnation? In other words, you were now done with this school called earth and ready to move on to a place where there is no more sickness, no more debt, no unhappiness, no suffering, and no pain. Sounds pretty good, doesn't it? But what would you miss? Would you miss dancing, or holding your baby in your arms? Would you miss the sound of rain, or the waves as they crash against the sand? Would you miss pizza and chocolate cake, sex and all the physical sensory pleasures we enjoy here on earth?

Both questions call attention to the life we are currently living. Is it less than you hoped for? Are you taking for granted this magnificent opportunity you have been given to create the life you were born to live? What is missing in your life, and what would you change?

The White Angels share that, **"Your life is the total accumulation of every thought you think, so choose wisely."** In essence, we create our destiny one thought at a time. Our exterior world is a reflection of our interior world. In his book *Thinking and Destiny*, Harold Waldwin Percival states, "This law of thought is destiny… it means essentially, that thinking is the basic factor in shaping human destiny." Simply put, you are what you think.

If we think from our heart, guided by our higher self and following our intuition, our thoughts will manifest from the light. By law of attraction, our lives will be a reflection of that light.

"Your higher self is the fullness of you. It is the part of you that is perfectly aware of its divine nature and relationship to God. It is 'the watcher'… Your higher self is the soul-eternal and never-ending. Your lower self is the physical manifestation of the higher self. It is dense energy vibrating at a lower frequency. The lower self is often unaware of the higher self. However, once it is discovered it can access more of its light into the physical experience.

"With the knowledge and wisdom of the higher self to guide your physical experience, your true identity emerges. Your reason for being is made clear and your divine nature revealed. Intuition is the whisper from your higher self. Follow your intuition, your inner guidance system. It is the lighthouse on the stormy sea of life. Doubt not your inner guidance for it is the truest compass you possess. Ask then listen… listen then trust."

— The White Angels

I was born with scoliosis. My parents were wise and forward-thinking and put me in dance class at a very early age. It helped that my mother was a dance instructor and had her own school. Dance kept my body moving so the scoliosis never bothered me as a child or young adult. After a career in dance, I transitioned into a career in fitness, still moving my body. As the years crept along and I stopped teaching, I noticed that my back hurt if I didn't keep active. Because of my scoliosis, one hip was significantly higher than the other and the opposite shoulder was rotated and really out of whack. When my spine was out of alignment to the point of pain, I knew that I had to do more yoga, Pilates, Reiki, and schedule regular visits with a chiropractor to relieve it. Because I didn't want to suffer, I made sure I was consistent with exercise and care of my spine.

Why am I talking about scoliosis? Because aligning our lives to the vibration of love and joy relieves suffering, just as yoga aligns my spine. We come from joy, and we are made of joy. Love and joy are the very essence of who we are and why we are here. Somehow, we lose track of that along the way, and the drama of life clouds our heavenly perspective. But it doesn't have to be that way if we align with God and our higher self, trusting in our internal guidance system and listening to the angels.

"Align yourself to God. God is unconditional love and eternal joy. One can only feel happiness and ever-new joy when in alignment with God. Practice positive thinking and kindness. See the spark of God in all creation—every man, woman, and child. See God in every creature great and small. Find God in the sky, sun, moon, stars, trees, oceans, mountains, and deserts. Align yourself to Mother Earth and her grounding energy, feel her strength and love. Fill your heart with gratitude and thanksgiving. Give of yourself, share your talents and serve others. Be still. Be peaceful.

"When you are in alignment with God, you align yourself with the cosmos and the vibration of creation. When you are aligned with God you will feel it in your heart, you will know it in your soul. The floodgates of the universe will open and abundant blessings will pour down upon you. Aligning to God's vibration of unconditional love and joy awakens the soul to experience life as it was intended. Experience the sweetness life has to offer and fill your days in awe of the miracles that surround you. Receive fully the abundant blessings of happiness and joy when aligned with the Creator."

—The White Angels

God is not dependent upon us to believe in His/Her existence. You will align with the vibration of God energy every time you help your neighbor or speak kind words to a stranger. Being in nature aligns you. Imagine how you feel standing on a cliff overlooking the breathtaking view of the Grand Canyon or walking on the beach during a magnificent sunset. When your heart is bursting with joy and gratitude as you watch your child take her first step or speak his first word, you are aligned. Gratitude is the ultimate alignment to God's energy.

God is not out there looking down at us from His/Her heavenly throne as many of us have been taught. God does not judge our every action and condemn us to the throws of hell and damnation if we sin. We are not sinners. God is not separate from you or me. This is the higher law of unity. It was the first law Moses was given but the masses were not ready to receive its simplicity, so he came back down the mountain a second time with the Ten Commandments. It was the message Jesus Christ came to deliver when he said, "That they all may be one; as thou, Father, art in me, and I in thee, that they also may be one in us: that the world may believe that thou has sent me" (John 17:21). The White Angels share that the law of unity is the most important law of the universe: **"all things are part of the One."** We are not separate from God, nor are we separate from each other.

> "The most important law of the universe is the law of unity. The law of unity is a law of one. God is unconditional love and this is God's highest law. Humankind must unite together as one family, for all are God's children equally and one in God. When you embrace this law fully and completely, you are ready to go to the light. Your heart must be cleansed of everything but the vibration of love for all of God's creation, all creatures great and small. Your hearts must be pure and cleansed with Christ consciousness.

> "Soften your hearts for one another. See the spark of God in all of your brothers and sisters and all living creatures. Show kindness and compassion to all. Look upon your neighbor as you look upon yourself for they are a reflection of the Divine. Rejoice in your oneness as a cosmic family and share your gifts and blessings with one another. Spread this message of love and unity to all and live it fully and completely."
> — The White Angels

The law of unity, or law of oneness, states that everything that exists emanates from one and the same source, and everything is connected to everything else. We are not separate from each other, nor are we separate from the world around us. Great mystics and sages of antiquity have known this God consciousness dwells within each of us and in all things. The ancient philosopher, Hermes Trismegistus, wrote in *The Kybalion,* "While All is in THE ALL, it is equally true that THE ALL is in ALL. To him who truly understands this truth hath come great knowledge."

Hermes taught that "The All" is imminent in every particle of the universe. Some refer to this all-encompassing Source as universal consciousness. Science is now catching up with this concept as noted by physicist Fred Alan Wolf: "Armed with the ancient knowledge and the modern vision that comes from modern physics, particularly quantum physics, we can rediscover what the ancients may have known. All we need are a few basic concepts—a new way of seeing the old way." Bruce Lipton, an American scientist, continues with this theory: "The new physics provides a modern version of ancient spirituality. In a universe made out of energy, everything is entangled; everything is one."

Considered a pioneer of the new paradigm of science called science within consciousness, Dr. Amit Goswami lectured on tangled hierarchies when I was at the Sivananda Ashram. He said, "You are not your brain, your brain is a tool that you use in the physical world, but it isn't you. It is an object in your consciousness. Your consciousness is the subject. The world is made of consciousness, the world is consciousness, quantum physics makes this as clear as daylight."

> "The universe is consistent. All systems function
> on the same principles, from the smallest cells
> in the body to the largest galaxies. They are all
> mere thoughts of God. These systems function by
> universal laws that are never changing. From the
> circulatory system in your body to the rotation of
> the planets around the sun, everything functions in

perfect order according to these universal laws.

"To better understand God, one must understand
God's laws. Learning these universal laws and
understanding them leads to an accelerated and
joyful life. One who knows the universal laws and
is in tune with them vibrates at a higher frequency.
All things appear different from the external
perspective, but this is not true. Everything is the
same, all things are connected, and everything that
exists are mere thoughts of God."
— The White Angels

Once we grasp the understanding that we are not separate
from Source or from everything else, our awareness expands
from the lower self to the higher self. This expansion allows
us to look beyond our own self-interests to the world around
us. Our focus is no longer limited to our individual needs
and wants but considers our global family. The angels are a
part of this family. It is their responsibility to help us love
and care for each other, and by doing so, live a happier,
healthier life.

"The law of unity is the basis of all things, yet few
understand this law. When you live a life believing
you are separate from others, you live apart from
the law of unity. When one can love all things
equally, one has achieved the highest goal. Look
upon others as a spark of the Divine, and open your
heart to love as God loves.

"The great ascended masters came to teach this law.
Humankind is not separate from the smallest ant
that crawls upon the earth or from the largest star
in the galaxy. To feel that you are one with all is to
understand the law of unity. To respect all that is

not you, which in reality is the very essence of you,
is to understand this law."
— The White Angels

Our individual consciousness is a part of the greater consciousness like a wave is a part of the ocean. We feel our individuality, and yet, like the wave, the ocean is in every part of us. The only way to access the ocean of universal consciousness is to leave our five sense perceptions and immerse ourselves in the deep waters of meditation. When we lift our gaze to the point between the eyebrow (the third eye) and focus on the light within, combined with chanting the sacred sound of OM, we gain passage to the world beyond this physical realm, the cosmic world where angels fly. The White Angels say, **"With the alchemy of pure light and sound, one can access the all-inclusive, universal consciousness."**

Light and sound is a powerful combination, as Archangel Metatron demonstrated one morning during a meditation. He showed me a shape and called it my personal sacred geometry. Then he gave me a sound to accompany the shape. Archangel Metatron then instructed me to sit in meditation and visualize myself surrounded by this sacred geometry while chanting the sound. He explained that each of us have our own individual sacred combination of geometry and sound that when activated together increases our DNA strands and allows us a greater ability to comprehend the mysteries and secrets of the universe.

Rose VanDen Eynden validates this concept in her book *Metatron: Invoking the Angel of God's Presence*. VanDen Eynden writes, "Ancient scholars believed that by studying sacred geometry and meditating on its patterns, inner knowledge of the Divine and our human spiritual progression can... be gained." Eynden believes that studying sacred geometry "leads one to an understanding of how Creator has structured the physical world around us... shells, flowers, DNA molecule that is the building block of human life, and the galaxy itself in which Earth resides."

> "The superconscious mind holds information in your DNA. As your DNA expands and more strands are available to you, more information will become accessible. Additional strands of DNA are acquired as you raise your vibration on the path of ascension. Very few have this capability. Humankind would not understand the messages and in their ignorance would surely reject them. Those that have ears to hear..."
> — The White Angels

According to studies at the Institute of HeartMath in Boulder Creek, California, our DNA is influenced by factors like love and appreciation. The White Angels tell us that our strands of DNA increase as we raise our vibration on the path of ascension. Archangel Metatron gave me a tool that I now use to increase my vibration and expand my DNA. In chapter 11, the White Angels specifically outlined ten important steps we can take to raise our vibrations. I believe as the frequency of our vibration increases, so too does our ability to communicate with angels and heavenly beings.

We increase our frequency when we live in the vibration of love, appreciation, and joyfulness. However, this requires us to live in the moment. It has been said that living in the past brings fear and living in the future brings anxiety, so all we really have is the present moment. The White Angels share that we are here to live a life filled with unlimited joy. It is our birthright to experience joy in the moment.

Abraham Hicks says it beautifully: "Everything exists for joy. There is not one other reason for life than joy. We've got nothing to prove to anyone, because nobody other than All-That-Is is watching. In other words, we're not trying to get brownie points from some other galaxy. We're not trying to get someplace else; we're not trying to get it done, because there is no ending—we cannot get it done. Everything exists for the purpose of joy in the moment."

> "You came to this earth to experience joy. Joy is the very essence of Source. Joy is found in service to others. It is found in the process of creation and expansion. To be joyful is to be in alignment with God, Source, and the universal consciousness. Laugh, play, and be joyful as a child. Do not take this life too seriously, for it was not meant for suffering and pain.

> "Raise your vibration through awareness and positive thinking. Be kind to one another and love your neighbor. See THE ONE in all and everything. Find joy, live joy, be joy. You are powerful cocreators. Command your power and create the life you came here to live, a life filled with unlimited joy."
> — The White Angels

The White Angels explain that it is possible to create a joyful, happy atmosphere here and now. They call this Heaven on earth.

> "Heaven is here and now. Do not wait for Heaven, but create for yourself a heaven on earth. Live

your life as if you are in heaven communing with the angels and celestial beings. Are your earthly brothers and sisters not sons and daughters of God? Look beyond the delusion the world presents and see the beauty and the Divine in all things. In this way, you take heaven with you wherever you go.

"Fill your home with objects of high vibrations. Place pictures of ascended masters, saints, and angels in your home to remind you of Heaven. Listen to inspiring music, and fill your home with books of enlightenment, truth, and wisdom. Invite friends and loved ones into your home and communicate with love and kindness. Bring laughter and joy into your home. Pay homage to Mother Nature with plants and flowers placed lovingly in your home. Invite the angels in as guests in your home.

"Use caution when allowing negative words and ideas from others into your home through media or literature. This negativity will lower the vibration and cripple the spirit through fear. Speak the truth in your home, for there are no untruths spoken in Heaven. Practice living now what you wish to live beyond this lifetime. Surround yourself with beauty and wisdom and create a peaceful atmosphere in which to live. Ask God to bless your home with love and light."
— The White Angels

Let me ask you again... what would you do if this was your last year on earth? What changes would you make? What dreams would you realize and what imprint would you leave behind?

I hope after reading this book, you no longer feel alone

or unsupported by the universe. I hope it is clear that you do not have to be a saint, ascended master, or a rishi to access the angelic realm. If I can do it, anyone and everyone can.

You are surrounded, protected, guided, and loved by your angels. We are all one, divine sparks of God. Trust your intuition, and listen to the whispers of your angels. You are here to live a life filled with unlimited, ever-changing new joy, and your angels are here to help you realize that dream. Just ask.

Bibliography

The following is a list of books I found very helpful on my spiritual path. I hope you enjoy them as much as I did.

Autobiography of a Yogi by Paramahansa Yogananda, 1946

The Second Coming of Christ, The Resurrection of the Christ Within You-Paramahansa Yogananda, 1979

The Holy Science by Swami Sri Yukteswar, 1920

Meditation and Mantras by Swami Vishnu devananda, 1999

The complete book of Yoga by Swami Vishnu devananda, 1999

The Bagavad Gita by Sri Swami Sivananda, 2000

No Greater Love by Mother Teresa, 1995

Siddhartha by Hermann Hesse, 1922

Quantum Creativity by Amit GoSwami PhD, 2014

Jesus: The Explosive Story of the 30 Lost Years and the Ancient Mystery Religions by Tricia McCannon, 2016

The Keys to the Universe by Diana Cooper and Kathy Crosswell, 2010

A Dictonary of Angels-Including Fallen Angels by Gustav Davidson, 1967

The Essenes: Children of The Light by Stuart Wilson and Jonna Prentis, 2005

The Emerald Tablet of Hermes and the Kybalion, Two Classic Books on Hermetic Philosophy by Hermes Trismegistus, (1912, published by the Yogi Puglication Society of the Masonic Temple

Notes

Notes

Notes

Notes

Notes

Notes

Notes

Notes

Notes

Notes